Participation in God

Participation in God

A Forgotten Strand in Anglican Tradition

A. M. ALLCHIN

Darton, Longman and Todd
London

First published 1988 by
Darton, Longman and Todd Ltd
89 Lillie Road, London SW6 1UD

© 1988 A. M. Allchin

ISBN 0 232 51781 9

British Library Cataloguing in Publication Data

Allchin, A.M. (Arthur Macdonald), *1930–*
Participation in God.
1. Church of England. Christian doctrine
I. Title
230′.3

ISBN 0–232–51781–9

Phototypeset by
Input Typesetting Ltd,
London SW19 8DR
Printed and bound in Great Britain by
Anchor Brendon Ltd,
Tiptree, Essex

For Michael Ramsey
100th Archbishop of Canterbury
with gratitude, affection and respect

Contents

Preface   ix

1   Introduction   1

2   The Mystery of Endless Union: Richard Hooker and Lancelot Andrewes   7

3   Man as God and God as Man: Charles Wesley and Williams Pantycelyn   24

4   A Life which is both His and Theirs: E. B. Pusey and the Oxford Movement   48

5   The Co-inherence of Human and Divine   63

Notes   78

Index   83

Preface

This is a book which discusses the doctrine of *theosis* as we find it expressed in a number of representative Anglican figures in the past. Its three central chapters are an expanded version of the Gorman-Garrett lectures delivered in the University of Dallas in November 1984, at the joint invitation of the theology department of that Roman Catholic university, and the Anglican School of Theology, which operates on its campus. I am deeply grateful to Father Peter Phan, the head of the theology department, and to Father Lynn Bauman, Dean of the Anglican School, for the invitation to Texas and for the heart-warming hospitality which I received there.

The final chapter looks at the question in more contemporary terms, though again with reference to the witness of scripture and tradition. It also has a transatlantic origin, having grown from a lecture given for the Trinity Institute at its national conference in New York and San Francisco in 1983. My own sense of the relevance to our contemporary problems of the historical material which these chapters contain was greatly strengthed by the response which I found in audiences in three very different parts of the United States. It will be for readers to decide whether or not this book has made a case, first for recognising that the patristic adage 'God became man so that man might become God' is not so foreign to Anglican tradition as is commonly assumed, and then for acknowledging that this doctrine of *theosis* is in no way remote from the concerns of late-twentieth-century humanity but rather is of vital importance for any truly human living and thinking today.

A. M. ALLCHIN

1

Introduction

The central affirmation of Christian faith declares that God himself has entered into our human situation and in doing so has totally transformed it. In the early Christian centuries this affirmation was frequently expressed in the succinct form 'God became man so that man might become God'.[1] Such a statement necessarily implies that the Christian gospel cannot be simply fitted into the world as it now is. It involves its radical transformation. It means a revolution not only in our idea of God but also in our idea of humankind and of the world in which we live.

What is involved in such a transformation of the world and of our understanding of it? That is the subject which is treated in this book. The material of which it is made is largely historical. But its purpose is anything but antiquarian. It seeks to respond to contemporary issues; has life a meaning? Is there a God? Can we know him and love him? Can our life in this world find any ultimate purpose and fulfilment? Have the churches any truth to convey to us on these topics? We have to acknowledge that the churches have too often given people the impression that God is far away, hard to appease, impossible to approach. Too often we seem to have spoken about God, theorised about him without being able to bring men and women to any living apprehension of his presence and his power.

As a consequence many of our contemporaries in the last quarter of a century have given up all thought of the search for God. Others have turned to the East, to the religious traditions of Buddhism and Hinduism, in search of a saving knowledge of the ultimate truth of things, which would be able to transform their consciousness and reshape their life. They have abandoned the Christian tradition which seems only to talk about God without showing any way to realise his presence, and have turned to other ways of discipleship which offer an experienced knowledge of our union, our identity with him. Christianity, which contains at its heart a message about the reconciliation and union of humanity with God, seems to them no longer to convey the mystery of which it speaks.

At one level of course the age in which we live is one of constant transformations. At the level of technology the human race has risen to hitherto unimaginable heights. Outwardly many human beings are rich as they have never been before. But we are unhappily aware of the fact that while outwardly much has changed, inwardly things are much as they were. The problems of the injustice in human society, of the division between rich and poor, the problems of our inner disharmony and brokenness, our psychological and spiritual problems, remain or indeed seem to get worse. Certainly in Great Britain the scandal of economic injustice has been greatly sharpened in the last ten years. While in some ways our society is rich, in other ways it is notably poor. The poverty of content which characterises so much of what we show on our television screens is one example of this. The poverty of what we show contrasts forcibly with the sophistication of the machines we employ to show it. The message has disappeared in the elaboration of the media. When we turn to past ages, which were poor indeed in all that we call technology, when to get from one place to another you had to walk or at best ride on a horse, we sometimes discover a wealth of insight into the human heart, a wealth of understanding of the things of God which puts us to shame, or rather reminds us of our true inheritance, human and divine. We are not more perceptive than Shakespeare nor wiser than Hooker.

We shall then delve back into the past, in the conviction that in the Christian tradition there are resources of great significance for our own day; not ready-made answers to our contemporary problems, some of which are entirely new, but rays of illumination which can show us that our present position is neither so desperate nor so isolated as we are sometimes tempted to fear. The age in which we live suffers from the illusion that we are cut off from the past; hence our sometimes frenzied search for roots. But in reality the experience of the past is not far from us, and when that past is full of the power of the Holy Spirit it is also full of resources for our life, for eternal life which can become available for us today. Those who in the past have lived and prayed and thought through the mystery of Christ's dying and rising can, if we will let them, become our contemporaries through the gift of the Holy Spirit, who takes the things of Christ and makes them known to us.

More specifically we shall be looking into that area of the past which belongs in a particular way not only to England but also to the English-speaking world. I write as an Anglican, but I address not only my fellow Anglicans but any who would wish to share in this particular strand in the total, complex heritage of English-speaking Christians. So we shall be looking at the doctrine of deification as it is to be found in representative Anglican theologians during the last four centuries; that is, the doctrine not only that

God has come down to be where we are, in our human mess, but that he has lifted us up to be where he is in his divine splendour. To do this in itself requires a small revolution in our way of looking at things. For it is common knowledge that Anglicans do not hold this doctrine, and certainly do not use this terminology. As the Anglican-Orthodox Joint Doctrinal Commission pointed out in its Agreed Statement in Moscow in 1976, while the Orthodox speak of the fulness of man's sanctification in terms of his sharing in the life of God, using the term *theosis kata charin* (divinisation by grace), 'such language is not normally used by the Anglicans, some of whom regard it as dangerous and misleading'.[2]

A glance at some of the standard works on the Anglican theological and spiritual tradition makes this clear. We find no mention of the subject, for instance, in Martin Thornton's influential book, *English Spirituality* (1963). Indeed in that book the whole of the eighteenth- and nineteenth-century period – of William Law and Charles Wesley, of John Henry Newman and Edward Bouverie Pusey – is covered in a brief chapter called 'The Post-Caroline Disintegration'. It is a title which hardly encourages further research into the field. Turning to a more recent study, J. R. H. Moorman's *The Anglican Spiritual Tradition* (1983), a work which is entirely devoted to the post-Reformation period, we find a similar situation. True enough the book contains references to Charles Wesley's hymns and to Pusey's sermons, but very little is said as to why such works deserve mention in the history of Anglican spirituality, let alone in the spiritual tradition of Christendom as a whole. The genuinely mystical quality of the theology of these two writers is scarcely hinted at.

For it is also common knowledge that the English are a nation of shopkeepers. They do not produce mystics. Julian of Norwich, George Fox, William Blake, not to mention the writers discussed in this book, are not part of their tradition. At least they are not part of our customary way of understanding that tradition. Just as in a psychological illness a person may find themselves cut off from large areas of their own past, so it seems that the English today have great difficulty in recognising large parts of their own inheritance. If we are to understand ourselves better, if we are to find a way out of our present *impasse*, we shall have to learn to look at things in our own history in a new perspective. We shall have to take seriously the subtitle which Nicholas Lossky has given to his study of the theology of Lancelot Andrewes, 'the origins of the mystical theology of the Church of England' (*aux sources de la théologie mystique de l'Eglise d'Angleterre*). Perhaps after all we have such a theology, though we are scarcely aware of it.[3]

To make such an acknowledgement has immediate consequences

for our social as well as our personal existence. It is well known that the category of the personal is vital to Christian thinking, both in relation to God who is understood to be three-personed and to humanity which is seen as made in God's image and likeness. Often in common usage what is personal is thought to be identical with what is individual. But the reverse is the case. For whereas when we speak of the individual we speak of each one in his separateness in competition with all others, when we speak of the person we speak of each one in his relatedness, in communion with all others. Indeed just as in God each of the three divine persons lives in and through the others, so also it is at the human level. We are members one of another. In each the whole is present. Consider what Pusey says, referring back to John Chrysostom:

> The joy which God has in the redemption of the world, he has in the conversion of a single soul, and we owe as deep a debt of love, as though he had come for us alone: yea, deeper far since the salvation of others is our gain, not his; for the bliss of all shall increase the bliss of each, while each in each beholds the glory of God reflected, and in the glory of each shall we have our own special joy.[4]

There is nothing privatised about this intimately personal joy.

The joy which God has in his creation and creation's responding joy in God is one of the underlying themes of this book, which is taken up explicitly in Chapter 5 on the co-inherence of human and divine. In the preceding three chapters, which form the core of the work, we look at the subject of our participation in the life of God, as we find it treated in the seventeenth century by Hooker and Andrewes, in the eighteenth by Charles Wesley and Pantycelyn, and in the nineteenth by Pusey and Keble. In all we are conscious of a movement of awestruck joy at the presence of God with us and in us, an experience of the dynamic joy of the kingdom which changes all things, overthrowing our customary ways of thinking of the relationships of God with man. From this centre of amazement we gain a new way of looking at things, an alteration of consciousness, a realisation that we are able to respond to the world's problems when we see that in the power of the gospel the problems themselves are being changed and that we ourselves are in the process of changing.

It is of this joy that the American Orthodox theologian Alexander Schmemann spoke, in a remarkable lecture given in Oxford towards the end of his life, a lecture which summed up many of the concerns which had been with him throughout his ministry:

4

We cannot answer the world's problems by adopting towards them an attitude either of surrender or of escape. We can answer the world's problems only by changing those problems, by understanding them in a different perspective. What is required is a return on our part to that source of energy, in the deepest sense of the word, which the Church possessed when it conquered the world. What the Church brought into the world was not certain ideas applicable simply to human needs, but first of all the truth, the righteousness, the joy of the Kingdom of God. The *joy* of the kingdom; it always worries me that, in the multivolume systems of dogmatic theology that we have inherited, almost every term is explained and discussed except the one word with which the Christian Gospel opens and closes . . .[5]

And Schmemann goes on to argue that it is only when the joy of the kingdom finds its place again at the centre of theology, that theology will be able in a constructive way to speak to the whole of the human situation today. For this joy is a sign of the gratuitousness and transcendence or the gift of God, which always goes beyond anything we could ask or think, yet at the same time really makes itself known to us, with us and in us, constantly surprising us by its unlooked-for fulfilment of the deepest longings of the human heart and mind.

It is the contention of this book that the doctrine of our deification, our becoming partakers of the divine nature by God's grace, is inseparably and necessarily bound up with the other two doctrines which stand at the heart of classical Christian faith and life, the doctrine of God as Trinity, and the doctrine of the incarnation of God the Word. All three doctrines belong together, and it may be our neglect of the one which has made us uncertain about the others. It is very striking that when the fathers of the Church, Athanasius, Gregory Nazianzen or Cyril of Alexandria, for instance, wish to prove the divinity of the Holy Spirit, they turn at once to the fact that the Spirit makes us truly sharers in God's nature, makes us sons in the Son, temples of God. We know that the Spirit is God because he makes us participant in God. There is an immediate appeal to experience. The doctrine of God as Trinity is intended to safeguard both the transcendence of God and his immanence. God who is utterly beyond his creation yet comes to be present at the heart of his creation comes to identify himself with his creation in order to lift it up into union with himself. This union, established once for all in the person of Christ, is constantly renewed in varying ways in the coming of the Spirit.

Many of our current controversies in Christology seem to stem from an inadequate understanding of the doctrine of God, an understanding which does justice neither to his total transcendence nor to his total immanence. Corresponding to this inadequate vision of God there stands an equally inadequate vision of our human nature. We no longer see our humanity as created for union with God, capable of being made one with God, called to be the place of God's indwelling. Without the doctrine of our deification by grace the doctrine of the incarnation in the end loses its meaning and finality. For how can God enter into man unless man is made from the beginning to enter into God?

It is true that the explicit affirmation that we are made partakers of the divine nature occurs only once in the New Testament (2 Pet. 1:4). But the Pauline teaching about our incorporation into Christ through the work of the Holy Spirit, and the Johannine teaching about God's dwelling in us and we in him, both affirm that the Christian 'is taken into a relation of unlimited intimacy with God'.[6] Throughout the New Testament a co-inherence of human and divine is implied, a relationship of union and communion which overthrows our customary ways of thinking both of God and humankind, and opens the way towards the wonder of our adoption into the circulation of the divine life. This faith and experience is not something peripheral to the New Testament writings. It is at their heart.

It is similarly at the heart of the faith of the Church both in East and West for at least the first millennium of the Christian era. In the West we might think of a simple expression of it in the prayer which accompanies the mingling of the water with the wine at the Eucharist, in which we pray that as God became partaker of our human nature so may we become partakers of his divine nature. In the East this doctrine has remained more clearly at the centre of the Church's teaching. Indeed many would regard it as being one of the distinguishing marks of Eastern Orthodoxy. As John Meyendorff points out in his classic study of Byzantine theology, it has many consequences for our understanding both of human and divine nature: 'Man, while certainly a creature and, as such, external to God, is defined in his very *nature* as being fully himself only when he is in *communion* with God.' To become fully human, to realise our human potential, we need to enter into communion with our Creator. We can become ourselves only by transcending ourselves. He that will find his life must lose it. There is nothing static about this communion. It is the beginning of a process which will lead us through death into life, life in this world and life in the world beyond this one, 'an eternal progress into the inexhaustible riches of the divine life.'[7]

2

The Mystery of Endless Union:
Richard Hooker and Lancelot Andrewes

Richard Hooker (1554–1600), author of *The Laws of Ecclesiastical Polity*, is in many ways the greatest Anglican theologian since the break with Rome, and the one who has had unrivalled influence in the development of our tradition. There is much about him which seems almost miraculous and is certainly difficult to explain. Living in the world of Elizabeth I, a world of enormous vitality and energy, of violent controversy and conflict, how did he manage to create a work so balanced and serene? How did he manage to see so far into his subject? Where did he get his capacity to trace back secondary issues to the hidden first principles which lie behind them? It is a work of theological reflection and analysis marked by a contemplative quality which we might have expected from someone living in a calmer and more secluded atmosphere than his. We are apt to think of London at the end of the sixteenth century as a place whose mood was secular, commercial, aggressively self-confident and expansionist, creative in music and in the theatre but hardly in theology and spirituality. It is from that world that Hooker and Andrewes emerge, and, as T. S. Eliot remarks, 'if the Church of Elizabeth is worthy of the age of Shakespeare and Jonson, that is because of the work of Hooker and Andrewes'.[1]

Hooker is a man who constantly seeks to hold together things which are easily set in opposition to one another, and which were in fact frequently contrasted with one another in the bitter controversies of the Reformation and the counter-Reformation; nature and grace, faith and reason, word and sacrament, scripture and tradition. Above all things he is concerned to hold together the glory of God and the true dignity of man. This means that in his controversial writings he finds himself defending the rights of human reason and experience over against the demands of a Calvinism which was already setting the sovereignty of God over against the freedom of man, thinking to exalt God at the expense of his creation. This was never Hooker's way. He sees God's wisdom and power shining out in and through all things, in the richness and diversity of the world which God has made, and above all in man whom he has created in his image and likeness.

7

I

In the admirable pages devoted to Hooker in the sixteenth-century volume of the *Oxford History of English Literature*, C. S. Lewis writes:

> Every great system offers us a model of the universe; Hooker's model has unsurpassed grace and majesty. From what I have already said it might be inferred that the unconscious tendency of his mind was to secularise. There could be no deeper mistake. Few model universes are more filled – one might say, drenched – with Deity than his. 'All things that are of God', and only sin is not, 'have God in them and they in himself likewise, and yet their substance and his are wholly different.' God is unspeakably transcendent; but also unspeakably immanent.

And Lewis goes on in a long and memorable paragraph to spell out what for Hooker is implied in this sense of the immanence of the transcendent God:

> All good things, reason as well as revelation, nature as well as grace, the commonwealth as well as the Church, are equally, though diversely, 'of God' . . . All kinds of knowledge, all good arts, sciences and disciplines come from the Father of lights and are 'so many sparkles resembling the bright fountain from which they rise' . . . We meet in all levels the divine wisdom shining out through 'the beautiful variety of all things' in 'their manifold and yet harmonious dissimilitude'.[2]

This picture of the whole creation as full of the energy and wisdom of God, which we find in Hooker, is of course in various different forms typical of the theology of both East and West, especially in the earlier centuries of the Christian era. All Christian thinking has been concerned to stress the absolute distinction between Creator and creation; no system which blurred that line would be considered as within the mainstream of Christian tradition. Yet the complementary balancing truth of God's presence in his world is no less necessary for a full understanding of Christian doctrine, and this side of the coin has often been neglected in more recent thinking, particularly in the West; perhaps this is one of the reasons why the doctrine of man's participation in God has fallen into the background. For to speak of man's participation in God, still more to speak of his deification, otherwise than in the context of a whole world which participates in God is to speak a non-sense. The doctrine of man's *theosis* can only make sense when seen in relation to a world filled, or rather drenched, with Deity, a world of which it is possible to say, 'The Word of God, who is God wills in all things and at all times to work the mystery of his embodiment.'[3]

Lewis's appreciation of Hooker's theology in this section of his book is profound and eloquent. It would be interesting to investigate how far his own outstanding ability as an expositor of Christian doctrine is rooted in his familiarity with one of the greatest Christian thinkers of the past. It is surely not an accident that Lewis was able to set out the basic common elements of the Christian faith, 'mere Christianity' as he calls it, in a way which avoids the temptation of a bland lowest common denominator and which still after forty years speaks to a multitude of Christians of very different traditions. In doing this he was following one of the basic intentions of Hooker's thought, that is, to distinguish what is necessary in Christian faith from what, however important it may be, is of secondary significance, and to show that in the fundamental doctrines Christians are more united than they think they are. It seems that the most widely read of Anglican writers in the twentieth century may have been more indebted than at first appears to the greatest of his sixteenth-century predecessors.

We have said that Hooker never denigrates man in order to exalt God. Let us see how it is that he will expound the nature of man, as a creature who though finite, sinful and mortal has planted within him a longing for what is infinite and immortal. We shall find that if he may rightly be claimed as a humanist, his is a very special theocentric humanism, a vision of man which finds its fulfilment in God.

No good is infinite [he writes], but only God; therefore he our felicity and bliss. Moreover desire leadeth unto union with what it desireth. If then in him we are blessed, it is by force of participation and conjunction with him. Again it is not the possession of any good thing that can make them happy which have it, unless they enjoy the thing wherewith they are possessed. Then are we happy therefore when fully we enjoy God, even as an object wherein the powers of our soul are satisfied, even with everlasting delight; so that although we be men, yet being into God united we live as it were the life of God.[4]

We note in this passage how our theme of deification is already foreshadowed in the phrase, 'although we be men, yet being into God united we live as it were the life of God'. We note too the use of two of Hooker's most characteristic terms, conjunction and participation, to describe the relationship of man to God. Still more we recognise in Hooker a calm affirmation about divine things which seems to come from an age other than our own, an age in which men looked into the things of God with more assurance than they do now, in which words like joy, happiness and delight easily have their place in the most serious theological discourse. Hooker seems to know with the whole of his being, not only with his massive and subtle intellect, that man is made for God and he can only find his fruition in him:

Complete union with him must be according unto every power and faculty of our minds apt to receive so glorious an object. Capable we are of God both by understanding and will; by understanding, as he is that sovereign Truth which comprehendeth the rich treasures of all wisdom; by will, as he is that sea of Goodness whereof whoso tasteth shall thirst no more. As the Will doth now work upon that object by desire, which is as it were a motive towards the end as yet unobtained, so likewise upon the same hereafter received it shall work also by love. '*Appetitus inhiantis, amor fruentis*', saith St Augustine. 'The longing disposition of them that thirst is changed into the sweet affection of them that taste and are replenished.' Whereas we now love that thing that is good, but good especially in respect of benefit unto us, we shall then love the thing that is good, only or principally for the goodness of beauty in itself. The soul being in this sort, as it is active, perfected by love of that infinite good, shall, as it is receptive, be also perfected with those supernatural passions of joy, peace and delight. All this endless and everlasting.[5]

Whereas the understanding grasps God as truth, the will grasps God as goodness, acting now by desire and looking towards the gifts which God will give. In eternity this longing will be turned into a pure disinterested joy in 'the goodness of beauty in itself'. We shall find this distinction worked out again more fully in a moment. But for the present leaving aside the details of Hooker's analysis of the movement of man's heart and mind, we are struck again by his assurance that placed at the centre of man's being, where will, thought and love meet and are at one, there is this longing for something greater than this world. Man is a creature whose nature it is always to seek that which is beyond his nature. He is a creature made for self-transcendence. His heart is restless till it can find its rest in God. This restlessness Hooker describes with great perceptiveness.

For man doth not seem to rest satisfied, either with fruition of that wherewith his life is preserved, or with performance of such actions as advance him most deservedly in estimation; but doth further covet, yea often-times manifestly pursue with great sedulity and earnestness, that which cannot stand him in any stead for vital use; that which exceeds the reach of sense; yea somewhat above the capacity of reason, somewhat divine and heavenly, which with hidden exultation, he rather surmiseth than conceiveth; somewhat he seeketh, and what that is directly it knoweth not, but very intentive desire thereof doth so incite, that all known delights and pleasures are laid aside, they give place to the search of this but only suspected desire.[6]

Not C. S. Lewis himself could be more eloquent in describing the power of this longing in man for something beyond, this 'very intentive desire', this passionate yearning for something only glimpsed and guessed at. This theme so powerfully developed in the romantics of the nineteenth century has its roots much further back in both the Greek and the Jewish origins of our tradition. Man seeks what is beyond him, but his desire remains baffled. He is thrown back on himself by the enigmas of sin and suffering, of frustration and death. Of himself he cannot attain the goal for which he longs. It is only when another comes out from the unknown world of eternity to meet him, and opens to him the way through, that man can find the fulfilment of the desire which he knows within himself. In Christ God himself comes out to meet man and becomes the way which leads into the kingdom of heaven. Here the initiative is God's; as Hooker says, 'The first thing is the tender compassion of God respecting us drowned and swallowed up in misery; the redemption out of the same by the precious death and merit of a mighty Saviour which hath witnessed of himself saying, "I am the way", the way that leadeth from misery to bliss.'[7]

What is involved for man as he follows this way into participation in the life of God is a constant growth into the three theological virtues or powers of faith, hope and love, a growth which leads us slowly from this world of time into the great world which lasts for ever. Of this journey Hooker speaks in memorable terms:

Concerning faith, the principal object whereof is that eternal verity which hath discovered the treasures of hidden wisdom in Christ; concerning hope, the highest object whereof is that everlasting goodness which in Christ doth quicken the dead, concerning charity, the final object whereof is that incomprehensible beauty which shineth in the countenance of Christ the Son of the living God; concerning these virtues, the first of which beginning here with a weak apprehension of things not seen, endeth with the intuitive vision of God in the world to come;

11

the second, beginning here with a trembling expectation of things far removed as yet but only heard of, endeth with the real and actual fruition of that which no tongue can express; the third beginning here with a weak inclination of the heart towards him unto whom we are not able to approach, endeth with endless union, the mystery whereof is higher than the reach of the thoughts of men . . .[8]

While faith apprehends God as truth and hope grasps him as life-giving goodness, love can in the end see in him only the ineffable beauty which shines in the countenance of Christ, a beauty with which we are to be conjoined in a mysterious union which goes beyond the thoughts of man. In saying this Hooker tells us much about his vision of God, as the supreme reality in whom goodness, truth and beauty are fused into one. But he tells us also much about his vision of man. While recognising the extreme fragility and weakness of his present state, the slowness of his development, he sees him as a creature of an infinite potential. The theological virtues are in some sense natural to him. He can grow into faith and hope and love, in a way which is at once both human and divine. He can come to share in the object of his love.

On this theme of participation in the divine beauty C. S. Lewis says in his sermon, 'The Weight of Glory':

We do not want merely to *see* beauty, though, God knows, even that is bounty enough. We want something else which we can hardly put into words – to be united with the beauty we see, to pass into it, to receive it into ourselves, to bathe in it, to become part of it . . . At present we are on the outside of the world, on the wrong side of the door. We discern the freshness and purity of the morning, but they do not make us fresh and pure. We cannot mingle with the splendours we see. But all the leaves of the New Testament are rustling with the rumour that it will not always be so. Someday, God willing, we shall be let in.[9]

Here again in twentieth-century terms and in the language of poetry, we glimpse a little of what is implied in the idea of participation, sharing in, becoming part of the very beauty and energy of God.

Olivier Loyer, in his fine and detailed analysis of the thought of Richard Hooker, speaks of Hooker's vision of man as of 'a being whose end is God himself', a being inhabited by 'a natural desire for a supernatural end'.[10] He shows how for Hooker the concept of participation becomes a key to be used to unlock many different areas of theological thought 'not only the economy of creation, but also the Trinitarian economy and the economy of salvation. In the heart of the Trinity, participation becomes procession of the persons, the circumincession, underlining at once their distinction and their mutual co-inherence. At the level of redemption it expresses the mystery of our adoption . . .' God is in us, we are in him by way of a mutual participation, in which creature and Creator remain distinct while being no longer separate. In Hooker's system:

> Participation stresses at once the transcendence and the immanence of God. At the level of creation, God is in us, hidden at the centre of our being, precisely because he creates this being from nothing and is thus intimately exterior to it. At the level of redemption precisely because he gives us his grace, and in so doing, reveals his complete sovereignty. This is the paradox of Christianity, difficult to grasp but essential. It is the very paradox of gift. Being and grace are truly ours because God really communicates them to us; they are not simply lent to us. And yet they are not ours, for they do not belong to us by our own right.[11]

Following this line of thought, as Loyer points out, Hooker tries to find his way through some of the most fiercely controverted questions of the sixteenth century. Grace truly becomes ours and truly transforms us; it is not merely imputed to us. But in so far as it is grace, God's free unmerited gift, we can never claim it as our own. As soon as we do so we break the link between the gift and the one who gives it. Following this line of thought and working within the terminology of the western scholastic tradition, Hooker opens up the way for a reaffirmation of the patristic conviction that man can indeed become partaker of the divine nature, but only and always by gift and grace, never by right and nature.

What this implies theologically Hooker spells out in a later section of his great work, in which he treats of the doctrine of the Church and the sacraments on the basis of a reaffirmation of the Christology of Chalcedon. Here again the concept of participation is essential:

> Sacraments are the powerful instruments of God to eternal life. For as our natural life consisteth in the union of body with soul, so our life supernatural in the union of the soul with God. And forasmuch as there is no union of God with man without that mean between both which is both, it seemeth requisite that we first consider how God is in Christ, then how Christ is in us, and how the sacraments do serve to make us partakers of Christ.

In other things we may be more brief, but the weight of these requireth largeness.[12]

This is the basis of the detailed exposition of what it means that we should be called to live the life of God, and to share in Christ as members of his body, which occupies the later part of his work. It is an exposition which at one point Hooker sums up in terms of the most familiar Trinitarian formula of the New Testament.

Life, as all other gifts and benefits groweth originally from the Father, and cometh not to us but by the Son; nor by the Son to any of us in particular but through the Spirit. For this cause the apostle wisheth the church of Corinth 'The grace of our Lord Jesus Christ, and the love of God, and the fellowship of the Holy Ghost,' which three St Peter comprehendeth in one, 'The participation of the divine nature.'[13]

Half a century later, towards the end of the civil war, preaching before the House of Commons in circumstances which Hooker could scarcely have envisaged, Ralph Cudworth placed the same doctrine at the centre of his presentation of the Christian message. By the time at which this sermon was preached the theological controversies already heated in Hooker's time had reached a new pitch of violence. Cudworth's statement is the more noteworthy for the background against which it is made. It is striking too that a thinker in many ways very different from Hooker, a representative of a different school of thought, philosophically speaking, should have made this same affirmation. One could not have a clearer indication of the influence of patristic thinking on the mainstream of Anglican theology.

And though the Gospel be not God, as he is on his own brightness, but God veiled and masked to us, God in a state of humiliation and condescendent as the sun in a rainbow, yet it is nothing else but a clear and unspotted mirror of divine holiness, goodness, purity, in which attributes lie the very life and essence of God himself. The Gospel is nothing else but God descending into the world in our form and conversing with us in our likeness that he might allure and draw us up to God and make us partakers of his divine form, *theos gegonen anthrōpos* (as Athanasius speaks) *hina hēmas en eautō theopoiēsē*; 'God was therefore incarnated and made man that he might deify us'; that is (as St Peter expresseth it) *makes us partakers of the divine nature.*[14]

14

II

We have looked at the teaching of Richard Hooker as we find it set out in his great work on *The Laws of Ecclesiastical Polity*. We turn to his contemporary, Lancelot Andrewes (1556–1626), together with him one of the most influential figures in the development of the Anglican communion since the Reformation. Andrewes was for more than twenty years preacher at the court of King James I. Year by year at Christmas, Easter and Whitsun he expounded the mysteries of the faith which the feasts celebrate. Year by year he summoned his auditors themselves to share in the gift of God offered to them first in the preaching of the Word then in the sacrament of Christ's body and blood celebrated at the altar. If in the case of Hooker we have a reflective, analytical style of theology continuing many of the methods of western scholasticism, in Andrewes' sermons we have a kerygmatic and liturgical theology, a theology of praise and proclamation, whose models are patristic rather than medieval. It is a theology which reaffirms and re-presents in London in the first twenty-five years of the seventeenth century that particular synthesis of dogma and experience, of thought and intuition, of learning and devotion which we find in the fathers of the first ten centuries, alike in East and West. This patristic quality has often been noticed in Andrewes' preaching, though some have thought that it was more a matter of external application, of laborious scholarship, than a living part of his thought. Such a supposition has been convincingly refuted in a recent study of Andrewes' theology, the work of a distinguished Russian Orthodox scholar teaching in Paris. Writing from within the eastern Christian tradition, and analysing Andrewes' teaching in detail and in depth, Nicholas Lossky shows in the preaching of the seventeenth-century bishop a living and dynamic presence of that understanding of the mystery of Christ which is characteristic of the teaching of the fathers, and especially of the fathers of the East.

One of the qualities of this teaching which has long been recognised is Andrewes' striking way of showing the connections between one doctrine and another, demonstrating the coherence of Christian theology. J. B. Mozley, writing in the *British Critic*, commented on this in the days of the Oxford Movement:

His theological explanations show the connection of one great doctrine with another, the bearing of one great fact of Christianity upon another, with admirable decision and completeness. He is so quick and varied, so dextrous and rich in his combinations; he brings facts, types, prophecies and doctrines together with such rapidity; groups, arranges, systematises, sets and resets them with such readiness of movement, that he seems to have a kind of ubiquity, and to be everywhere and in every part of the system at the same time . . . He has everything in his head at once; not in the sense in which a puzzle-headed person may be said to have, who has *every idea confused* in his mind because he has *no one idea clear*, but like a man who is at once clear-headed and manifold . . . in his ideas, who can do more than apprehend one point clearly or many dimly – can apprehend, that it to say, many keenly.[15]

Allied with this capacity to see and articulate the interaction of one element of faith with another there is a quality of depth or intensity in his writing, which drew the attention and commanded the assent of one of the greatest poets of our own century, T. S. Eliot. In the small book of essays in which he announced his adherence to the Catholic faith, entitled simply, *For Lancelot Andrewes*, Eliot speaks of this quality in terms of 'relevant intensity':

When Andrewes begins his sermon, from beginning to end you are sure that he is wholly in his subject, unaware of anything else, that his emotion grows as he penetrates more deeply into his subject, that he is finally 'alone with the Alone', with the mystery which he is seeking to grasp more and more firmly. One is reminded of the words of Arnold about the preaching of Newman. Andrewes' emotion is purely contemplative; it is not personal, it is wholly evoked by the object of contemplation to which it is adequate; his emotion is wholly contained in and explained by its object.[16]

Here is a description of a man in whose work thinking and feeling have been fused together. It is as he penetrates into his subject, by an intense intellectual effort, that his feeling grows. Here is a description of a man in whom what is within, what is subjective, is wholly evoked by what is beyond, the object of his contemplation, in whom subjective and objective are thus reconciled and at one. Here is a man who has been totally absorbed by his subject, caught up into it, in a way which is more than metaphorical. It is not surprising that such a one should be able to speak to us about participation in the divine nature, for he speaks from experience.

If we take a passage from a sermon for Christmas, where he discusses the meaning of the name Emmanuel, God with us, we shall be able to see both these characteristics. There is the interconnection of the doctrines touched on, incarnation, adoption, deifi-

16

cation, the virgin birth of Christ, the new birth in baptism of the Christian, the action of the Holy Spirit as life-creating in both cases, the parallel of the womb and the font as the place of new life. There is also the total concentration of the preacher which enables him to say so much in so brief a space. God, he says, is with us:

> to make us that to God that he was this day to man. And this indeed was the chief end of his being 'With us'; to give us a *posse fieri*, a capacity, 'a power to be made the sons of God', by being born again of water and of the Spirit; for *Originem quam sumpsit ex utero Virginis posuit in fonte Baptismatis*, 'the same original that himself took in the womb of the Virgin to usward the same hath he placed for us in the fountain of baptism to Godward', well therefore called the womb of the Church *sustoichon* to the Virgin's womb, with a power given it of *concipiet et pariet filios* to God. So his being conceived and born the Son of man doth conceive and bring forth (*filiatio, filiationem*) our being born, our being sons of God, his participation of our human, our participation of his divine nature.[17]

Thus at Christmas God's Son becomes the son of Mary, so that the sons of men may become the sons of God. Here already is the marvellous interchange of human and divine which the whole Christian mystery celebrates. But this is only the beginning. Christmas leads us on to the feasts which follow it; it points forward to the still greater mystery of death and resurrection, where we see the divine–human interchange in a new and still more striking perspective. Here again at Easter there is a birth; this time new birth from the dead:

> A brotherhood we grant was begun at Christmas by his birth, as upon that day, for 'Lo, there was he born.' But so was he also at Easter; born then too, and after a better manner born. His resurrection was a second birth, Easter a second Christmas . . .
> By the *hodie genui Te* of Christmas, how soon he was born of the virgin's womb he became our brother, sin except, subject to all our infirmities; to mortality, and even to death itself. And by death that brotherhood had been dissolved, but for this day's rising. By the *hodie genui Te* of Easter, as soon as he was born again of the womb of the grave, he begins a new brotherhood, founds a new fraternity straight; adopts us, we see, anew again by his *fratres meos*; and thereby he that was *primogenitus a mortuis* becomes *primogenitus inter multos fratres*; when 'the first-begotten from the dead', then 'the first-begotten of many

brethren'. Before he was ours, now we are his. That was by the mother's side; so he ours. This is *Patrem vestrum*, the Father's side; so, we his. But half-brothers before, never the whole blood till now. Now by the Father and mother both, *fratres germani, fratres fraterrimi*, we can not be more . . . This day's is the better birth by far.[18]

This vision of the incarnation and the resurrection and of the link between them is typical of Lancelot Andrewes, and it could be paralleled, though in a very different idiom, in Richard Hooker. Taken together these two great teachers provided a basic structure of doctrine which was filled out in varying ways by Anglican theologians of subsequent generations. Nicholas Lossky, commenting on this vision of the coherence of Christian doctrine, remarks:

In the characteristic theological strategy of Andrewes' preaching, we have noticed that the Christmas sermons, treating of the doctrine of the incarnation, underline time and again the paradox of the God, who is beyond all the heavens, limiting himself so as to become fully man, consubstantial with us, becoming participant in the whole of our human nature, sin only excepted. In the Easter sermons, the accent is constantly placed on what we may call the corollary of this paradox; the suffering servant, who has reached the lowest point of the human condition, is almighty God, consubstantial with the Father, who with the Father created the world. In his resurrection, consequence of his consubstantiality with the Father, he remains fully consubstantial with man, and from this there flows new life and a new destiny for all creation. Thus Easter is above all the feast of the joy of spring time, a spring time for creation which has been made new and has become heir to an eternal destiny. The Easter preaching of Andrewes, resounding with the hope and joy of the Passion–Resurrection of Christ is certainly not new, in this respect, in the whole history of Christian preaching. However in the seventeenth century in England, it was a long time since tones such as these had been heard.[19]

What is even less characteristic of the times in which these sermons were preached is the stress which Andrewes lays on the person and work of the Holy Spirit, in his highly developed pneumatology. Here it must be confessed that Anglican theology has by no means always succeeded in keeping up with his insight and understanding. Perhaps here we see another of the reasons why the teaching on deification has also fallen into the background, because it is in relation to our participation in God that Andrewes is most concerned to develop his understanding of the work of the Holy Spirit.

This is a point which Nicholas Lossky makes with emphasis in his recent study, pointing to the profoundly Trinitarian nature of Andrewes' vision alike of Christian faith and life.

> The importance given to pneumatology in the theology of Andrewes is to be explained, in my view, by the stress which he puts on the deification of man as the supreme goal of the way of salvation. It is a question of the union of man with God in Christ by the Holy Spirit. If his theology is at once christological and pneumatological it is because in his vision of salvation he makes profoundly his own the image in which St Irenaeus speaks of the Son and the Spirit as 'the two hands of the Father'. This image expresses the complementarity, reciprocity, the unity and the distinction of the two Persons in the divine economy. At the same time and above all else, it demonstrates that the divine economy is the action of the Three Persons of the Holy Trinity. As we have seen, this is something which Andrewes never forgets.[20]

All this implies that the whole theology of Andrewes, as he sets it out in his sermons, in all the complexity of its articulation, has in the end a practical purpose. He calls his hearers to repentance and newness of life. He calls them to participate in the life and love of God offered to them in their relations with their fellow men, in the worship and discipline of the Church and in the inner journey of faith and prayer. The summons to salvation is nothing less than a summons to enter into the very life of God.

> The christology and the pneumatology of Andrewes serve an end which includes them both and implies that they remain complementary. The Holy Spirit reveals the divinity of the Son who is the image of the Father (2 Cor. 4:4). Man who becomes 'partaker of the divine nature' (2 Pet. 1:4) enters into communion with the common nature of the Three Persons as it manifests itself from the Father by the Son in the Holy Spirit. By the uncreated grace of the Holy Spirit, God, that is to say the Trinity, comes to dwell in man, and man comes, if one can so say, 'in the Spirit by the Son, to the Father'. Thus one sees that if the theology of Andrewes is at once christological and pneumatological, it is above all trinitarian. And the trinitarian theology of Andrewes is, exactly like his christology and pneumatology, essentially directed towards the salvation of man . . .[21]

These points could be illustrated many times over from the sermons of Andrewes. Perhaps a passage from the opening of one of the Pentecost sermons will serve our purpose best. The preacher speaks of the difficulty of making any comparison between the work of Christ and the work of the Spirit, the gift of Christmas and the gift of Penecost.

These if we should compare them, it would not be easy to determine whether is the greater of these two: (1) that of the Prophet, *Filius datus est nobis*; or (2) that of the Apostle, *Spiritus datus est nobis*; the ascending of our flesh, or the descending of his Spirit; *incarnatio Dei*, or *inspiratio hominis*; the mystery of his incarnation or the mystery of our inspiration. For mysteries they are both, and 'great mysteries of godliness' both; and in both of them 'God is manifested in the flesh'. In the former by the union of his Son; in the latter by the communion of his blessed Spirit. But we will not compare them, they are both above all comparison. Yet this we may safely say of them: without either of them we are not complete, we have not our accomplishment; but by both we have, and that fully, even by this day's royal exchange. Whereby, as before he of ours, so now we of his are made partakers. He clothed with our flesh, and we invested with his Spirit. The great promise of the Old Testament accomplished, that he should partake of our human nature; and the great and precious promise of the New, that we should be *consortes divinae naturae*, 'partake his divine nature', both are this day accomplished.[22]

In such a passage we can see very clearly how much our western Christianity has lost through its failure to maintain the full complementarity and reciprocity between the work of Christ and the work of the Spirit. The once for all character of the work of Christ has been emphasised without any corresponding emphasis being given to the continuing work of the Spirit. As a result the work of Christ has come to be seen more and more simply as an event in the past. Its eternal dimensions have been lost to view. And that event in itself has been thought of more in terms of salvation *from* than salvation *for*. Good Friday has come to overshadow Easter. This can be seen in the way in which in Catholicism and Protestantism alike, the mass, the Lord's supper, has been thought of almost exclusively in terms of Christ's sacrificial death. The understanding of the Eucharist as the perpetual presence of Easter in the Church, the constant renewal of Pentecost, is a rediscovery of the last forty years. It is a striking fact that in the recent growth of agreement and understanding about eucharistic doctrine, the increased appreciation of the presence and activity of the Holy Spirit in the sacraments has played a crucial role. And this presence of the Spirit applies to the life of the Church as a whole. It was part of the inspiration of John XXIII to see the Second Vatican Council as a renewal of Pentecost. The same theme comes out strongly in the preaching of the present Pope, particularly during his visit to Poland at Whitsun 1979, where the upper room at Pentecost seems to open out into the foundation of the Church in Poland, into the baptism in the Spirit of the history and language of John Paul II and his fellow countrymen.

Andrewes goes further and declares that on the mystery of the *incarnatio Dei*, the incarnation of God, there follows a corresponding mystery, the *inspiratio hominis*, the in-spiration of man. The once for all event of the birth of Christ finds its fulfilment in the ever-renewed process of the coming of the Spirit. Both in the life of the Church and in the life of each member of the Church, progress and change are as necessary as fidelity and stability. Only in the unpredictable and infinitely varied action of the Spirit who is God and Lord and giver of life, and who moves with sovereign freedom throughout the affairs of men, do we begin to see the riches of God's glory and God's wisdom revealed. Only thus do we see how it is that while the history which led up to Jesus was full of the promise of his coming, the history which follows from him is full of an even greater and more mysterious expectation, the coming of the Spirit to dwell at the very heart of humanity and of all creation. The whole movement tends towards this in-spiration of man, this taking of humankind into the very life and being of the Triune God. We are caught up in a process as yet incomplete.

This aspect of the work of the Holy Spirit is fully developed in the preaching of Andrewes. A single quotation will give an example of it:

Now to be made partakers of the Spirit, is to be made 'partakers of the divine nature'. That is this day's work. Partakers of the Spirit we are by receiving grace, which is nothing else but the work of the Holy Ghost, the Spirit of grace. Grace into the entire substance of the soul, dividing itself into two streams; one goes to the understanding, the gift of faith; the other to the will, the gift of charity, the very bond of perfection. The tongues to teach us knowledge, the fire to kindle our affections. The state of grace is the perfection of this life, to grow still from grace to grace, to profit in it. As to go still forward is the perfection of a traveller, to draw still nearer and nearer to his journey's end.[23]

We are reminded at once of Eliot's lines, 'Not fare well, but fare forward, voyagers', and are stimulated to consider how all-pervasive the influence of Andrewes is in *Four Quartets*. But more importantly we notice the preacher's gift for summing up and resuming a whole burden of controversy in a single sentence. Grace is the breath of the Holy Ghost, the lifegiving activity of God penetrating into man in his totality, not a gift of God which could be dissociated from God but God himself at work in us, and if Andrewes speaks here of the soul, it is abundantly clear that he speaks of our nature as a whole for he sees man as a unity of body and soul, in-breathed, inspired by the Holy Spirit. And this activity of God creates 'the state of grace', which turns out, in a wonderful paradox, to be something eminently dynamic, to lead into a journey which has no end but God himself, who is without end, a journey which, as Hooker says, 'endeth with endless union', a still further penetration into the mystery of God which goes wholly beyond the thoughts of man. We are reminded again of T. S. Eliot, 'Old men ought to be explorers . . . We must be still and still moving into another intensity, for a further union, a deeper communion . . .'

To speak in such terms is to speak in the language of Christian mysticism, as Nicholas Lossky points out in the conclusion of his remarkable work. It is to speak that language, not as some esoteric or enclosed specialism, but as the full realisation of that which is offered to all in the mystery of the divine–human encounter in Christ and in the Spirit, the one fully and authentically catholic mystery of the love of God and the calling of man:

> The final goal of spiritual life being union with God, one can say that the theology of Lancelot Andrewes is a mystical theology, as long as one elucidates the meaning of the word 'mystical'. It is not a question of an exceptional experience, reserved for a few, in some way outside the traditional ways of theology. On the contrary it is a question of the interiorisation of the revealed Christian mystery, to which Andrewes calls all the baptised. This theology is mystical in the sense that it is not an abstract reflec-tion, but a concrete way of living the mystery in the deepening of the faith through prayer and the renunciation of one's own will. It is a way of the submission of the human to the divine will, which allows the grace of the Holy Spirit to impregnate human nature. For Andrewes it is altogether clear that this is only possible in fidelity to the given realities of revelation, that is to say in the scriptural and patristic tradition, or in other words in the catholicity of the Church.[24]

From what has been written in this chapter it will be clear that the question which we have been investigating, a question which to many would seem strange and esoteric, is in fact central to the theology of Hooker and Andrewes. Indeed it is central to their vision of Christian faith and life, since their theology is intended to subserve an eminently practical end, the living mystery of man's union with God in Christ, by the Spirit. As we shall see in the chapters which follow, the themes we have looked at here find their expression again in subsequent centuries, in the writings of a Charles Wesley who speaks of our being 'changed from glory into glory', or of an E. B. Pusey who preaches a sermon entitled 'Progress our Perfection'. We have looked back into the past to rediscover the tradition which we have received, and we find that it points us towards the future.

Man as God and God as Man:
Charles Wesley and Williams Pantycelyn

We have argued that the classical Christian doctrines of Trinity, incarnation and deification are much more closely related to one another than is commonly allowed, and we have tried to show something of the way in which those doctrines are linked together in two of the most authoritative representatives of the Anglican tradition in its post-Reformation form.

In this chapter we shall be looking at the work of two men who lived a century and a half later than Hooker and Andrewes, Charles Wesley (1707–88) and William Williams, Pantycelyn (1717–91), both leading figures in the Methodist or Evangelical movement of the eighteenth century. These were men who expressed their theology not primarily in books and sermons, though both were notable preachers and writers, but in the hymns they wrote. These hymns were written to be used by people who had been caught up into the movement in which they themselves were involved, hymns which had a great part in spreading and deepening that movement. Pantycelyn is universally recognised as the greatest of hymn writers in Welsh, and Charles Wesley has a good claim to be recognised as one of the two greatest hymn writers in English. They were both then outstanding figures in their own line of writing; but as hymn writers can they be seriously considered as theologians and still more can they be claimed as representatives of a tradition which may be called Anglican and Catholic? Were they not founding fathers of another tradition, the one which is called Evangelical?

To answer the second question first it must be said that it is one of the basic intentions of this book to question the way in which Evangelical and Catholic are commonly set in opposition to one another. The Evangelical Movement had, in its origins, profoundly Catholic intentions. The Oxford Movement in the nineteenth century had a profoundly Evangelical dimension at its heart. The two aspects of the one Christian tradition which in the West we have allowed to become separated from one another, and at times have made highly antagonistic, in fact need one another and complement one another. When we approach the theological differences between them by way of spirituality and worship, this fact becomes particularly evident as we shall hope to show. As to the first question, whether hymn writers can be theologians, I hope the present chapter will provide an answer. The fact that many of the hymns of the last two centuries have little real content and are simply expressions of pious emotions does not nullify the great tradition of theological hymn-writing in Christian East and West alike, a tradition which includes such men as St Ephrem, St John of Damascus and St Thomas Aquinas. Heart and head need not be set in opposition to each other. Indeed in worship they should be reconciled and united. A true hymn is neither simply a statement of doctrine nor simply an expression of devotion. It is a text in which thought and feeling, imagination and reason, have been fused together by the poet's craft and vision, through the gift of the Holy Spirit.

As far as the actual situation of the Methodist societies in the Church of England during the eighteenth century is concerned, it is well known that in England during the lifetime of the Wesleys there was no formal split. Both John and Charles Wesley died as they had lived, as priests of the Church of England. In Wales the final break with the Church came even later, in the early years of the nineteenth century. It is true that during the earlier period 'the people called Methodists' had already evolved their own structures and organisation within the framework of the established Church, and it may well be that on account of the rigidity of that Church and the lack of vision of its episcopate, a schism was in the end inevitable. But it was not something which the Wesleys wanted. It was only towards the end of his life that John Wesley began to ordain men for his work, first for America and then for Britain, and only after repeated requests to the bishops had been refused. It is noteworthy that his brother Charles never approved of these ordinations, and was adamant in his desire to die in communion with the Church of his baptism.

The seventeenth century both in Britain and in Europe had been a period of great religious fervour and theological creativity. Anglicans sometimes look back to the first half of that century as a kind of golden age which produced our greatest preaching in Andrewes, and our greatest poetry in George Herbert and Henry Vaughan. But it was also a century of fanaticism and violent religious conflict. On the continent of Europe there were wars of religion; there was the civil war in England. There was persecution and bitter polemic. Out of it all the eighteenth century emerged as an age of rationalism, moralism and scepticism, an age which saw the beginning of the modern rejection of the classical Christian tradition. Yet this same eighteenth century gave birth to its own religious movements, which were in reaction against the dominant tendencies of the time. There was a whole series of linked movements which on the Continent go by the name of Pietism and in the English-speaking world are called Evangelicalism or Methodism, and which were to have an immense influence on the religious life of the growing colonies of North America. They were movements of a fervent, deeply felt religion which called for individual conversion, and for a life which corresponded to the believer's profession of faith. They were movements which centred on the believer's personal encounter with Christ in a moment of experiential faith and forgiveness. It has often been thought that early Evangelicals were so concerned with their inner experience that they were no longer concerned with the traditional structures of Christian doctrine in Trinity, incarnation, deification, or with the traditional structures of Christian worship, above all of sacramental worship. Was the personal and individual element of Christian faith so underlined by them that they lost sight of the corporate nature of the Christian tradition as a whole? Let us turn to Charles Wesley and see what he will say.

I

Let earth and heaven combine,
　　Angels and men agree,
To praise in songs divine
　　The incarnate Deity,
Our God contracted to a span,
Incomprehensibly made man.

He laid his glory by,
　　He wrapped him in our clay;
Unmarked by human eye
　　The latent Godhead lay;
Infant of days he here became,
And bore the mild Immanuel's name.

Unsearchable the love
　　That hath the Saviour brought;
The grace is far above
　　Or man or angel's thought:
Suffice for us that God, we know,
Our God, is manifest below.

He deigns in flesh to appear,
　　Widest extremes to join;

To bring our vileness near,
  And make us all divine:
And we the life of God shall know,
For God is manifest below.

Made perfect first in love,
  And sanctified by grace,
We shall from earth remove,
  And see his glorious face:
Then shall his love be fully showed,
And man shall then be lost in God.[1]

Here we have a hymn which tells us of the incarnation of God the Word, a hymn particularly appropriate to Christmas. We notice at once the doctrinal, objective character of the first two verses, and the way in which they assume that the mystery of God's taking flesh is an event of universal, cosmic significance which will bring together heaven and earth, men and angels. But the doctrine being stated is not something abstract; it is constantly turning into worship. We not only delight in the paradoxes of faith but are stimulated by them to penetrate further into the mystery of God's coming to man. As so often with Charles Wesley there is consummate artistry in the use of words. The long latinate word *incomprehensibly* in the last line of the first verse contrasts with the short simple words which make up the previous lines. It tells us not only that we do not comprehend *how* it is that God enters into his creation, but that that action itself involves the comprehension of the incomprehensible. That which is unlimited enters our world of limitations. He who is from all eternity becomes a child. Eternity which surrounds us on every side enters into time, and in doing so bursts time open so that it becomes capable of receiving the divine. For, as we see in the subsequent verses, God does all this for our sake. He does it out of love in order 'to bring our vileness near, / And make us all divine'. Does the word 'all' here qualify 'us' or 'divine'? I think the latter, but we shall be able to judge better later. Here and now we are to know the life of God, and that knowledge will lead us onward to a fulness of life and vision in the world to come. 'Then shall his love be fully showed, / And man shall then be lost in God.'

It is a doctrinal hymn, but it is also an ec-static one, in the original meaning of that word which speaks of man's 'standing outside' himself. It shows us God coming out of himself to man and man being carried out of himself to God in response. It is both dogmatic and ecstatic in its language, and at the end Charles Wesley does not hesitate to speak of man's being lost in God. Such expressions might be thought to be dangerously pantheistic, to involve an improper idea of the merging of man in God. Such is not, I believe, Charles Wesley's intention. But as we shall see he is not afraid to use such language to underline the intimacy, the depth, the immediacy of the union of God and man in Christ, and in the believer who lives in Christ.

In such a hymn we see how the doctrine of the incarnation carries with it as a direct consequence the doctrine of man's deification. But nothing here is said explicitly about the role of the Holy Spirit. The Trinitarian framework is left unexpressed. To find this we may turn to another hymn addressed to the Holy Spirit:

> Come, Holy Ghost, all-quickening fire,
>   Come, and in me delight to rest;
> Drawn by the lure of strong desire,
>   O come and consecrate my breast;
> The temple of my soul prepare,
> And fix thy sacred presence there.
>
> Eager for thee I ask and pant;
>   So strong, the principle divine
> Carries me out, with sweet constraint,
>   Till all my hallowed soul is thine;
> Plunged in the Godhead's deepest sea,
> And lost in thine immensity.
>
> My peace, my life, my comfort thou,
>   My treasure and my all thou art;
> True witness of my sonship, now
>   Engraving pardon on my heart,
> Seal of my sins in Christ forgiven,
> Earnest of love, and pledge of heaven.
>
> Come then, my God, mark out thine heir,
>   Of heaven a larger earnest give;
> With clearer light thy witness bear,
>   More sensibly within me live;
> Let all my powers thine entrance feel,
> And deeper stamp thyself the seal.[2]

In general prayers addressed to the third person of the Trinity are not common in the Christian tradition. However, both in East and West such prayers can be found, prayers which ask the Holy Spirit to come and dwell in us, prayers which are widely used and strongly influential. In the Byzantine rite, for instance, there is the prayer, 'O Heavenly King, O Comforter'; in the Latin rite, the hymn 'Come Holy Ghost our souls inspire'. Wesley's hymn follows on in this tradition. It takes up thoughts which are present in these universally acknowledged petitions, and expresses them in a richly personal, lyrical vein. The first verse is remarkable for the way in which it speaks of God as being drawn to dwell in us by the lure of our longing for him. In writing thus Wesley attributes more to the element of human aspiration and desire than is common in the Reformation world, where the determination to maintain the priority of God's action has sometimes seemed to reduce man's part in the divine–human exchange almost to nothing. In the second verse we see that Wesley is not unmindful of this divine priority. It is the divine principle, the power of God within, which carries him out 'with sweet constraint' into union with the divine. The word 'constraint' brings with it overtones of St Paul in the second epistle to the Corinthians: 'the love of Christ constrains us' (2 Cor. 5:14). We are carried beyond ourselves by a divine love which establishes our freedom at the very moment in which it seems to take it away. We are taken into a union in which the soul becomes wholly God's. Here once again Charles Wesley employs language of great emphasis. We are plunged into the sea of the Godhead and lost in the divine immensity.

If this second verse speaks in the language of ecstasy, the third seems almost deliberately restrained in its use of biblical images. God is man's peace, man's life, man's comfort, his treasure and his all. The Spirit is the true witness to our sonship, who stamps the seal of Christ's forgiveness on our hearts, the earnest of God's love for us now, the pledge of its fulfilment in heaven. In the fourth verse these images are repeated but with a number of comparatives, 'larger', 'clearer', 'more sensibly', which suggest to us that the work of the Spirit is not something done within us once and for all, but something which is constantly to grow, 'from glory to glory', till all human powers feel the entrance of God's love and man receives the seal of the Spirit into the whole of his being.

Lest it should be thought that the language which we find in this hymn is exceptional in the usage of Charles Wesley it may be worthwhile to quote a short hymn from another of his collections, *The Hymns on the Lord's Supper*. Here the thought of the Church's eucharistic worship as containing a pledge or foretaste of the joy of heaven finds splendid expression:

> How glorious is the life above,
>   Which in this ordinance we taste;
> That fulness of celestial love,
>   That joy which shall for ever last!

That heavenly life in Christ concealed
   These earthen vessels could not bear;
The part which now we find revealed
   No tongue of angels can declare.

The light of life eternal darts
   Into our souls a dazzling ray,
A drop of heaven o'erflows our hearts,
   And deluges the house of clay.

Sure pledge of ecstasies unknown
   Shall this divine communion be;
The ray shall rise into a sun,
   The drop shall swell into a sea.[3]

This hymn forms one of a group on the theme of our present anticipation of the joys of heaven. As a group they have a particularly joyful quality to them. Christ himself, the true light, now darts a dazzling ray of his glory into our hearts and minds. A drop of the infinite ocean of divine joy overflows within us and deluges the house of clay. Not our souls alone but also our bodies are filled with the ecstasy of God. But all this is only a beginning. 'The ray shall rise into a sun,/The drop shall swell into a sea.' The words could not be simpler, the statement could not be more direct. We must recognise here the language of poetry. But to say that Charles Wesley is writing as a poet does not mean that we should take him with less than full seriousness. He means what he says, though we are to understand how he says it.

In the introduction to the *Large Hymn Book* which he published in 1780, John Wesley outlined his purpose in publishing this collection:

It is not so large as to be cumbersome or expensive: and it is large enough to contain such a variety of hymns as will not soon be threadbare. It is large enough to contain all the important truths of our most holy religion, whether speculative or practical . . . So that this book is, in effect, a little body of experimental and practical divinity.

The theological purpose of the collection could not be clearer. He goes on to defend the style and manner of the hymns, and he does so the more freely because the vast majority of them were not his own work but that of his brother.

Here nothing is turgid or bombast, on the one hand, or low and creeping on the other. Here are no *cant* expressions, no words without meanings. Those who impute this to us know not what they say. We talk common sense, both in prose and in verse, and use no word but in a fixed determinate sense. Here are, allow me to say, both the purity, the strength and the elegance of the English language; and at the same time the utmost simplicity and plainness, suited to every capacity.[4]

It is a noble declaration of the aims of a hymn writer. But surely John Wesley is overstating his case when he says, 'We talk common sense, both in prose and in verse'. Is that really true of those ecstatic expressions of Christian love? Is he not over-reacting in his desire to defend his brother's more passionate verses from the accusation of enthusiasm? Perhaps he is. But what he says here is more true than we might at first sight imagine. The words 'common sense' in eighteenth-century usage had a less wholly banal and reductive meaning than they have today. Dr Johnson in his life of Gray writes, 'I rejoice to concur with the common reader; for by the common sense of readers, uncorrupted by literary prejudices, after all the refinements of subtlety and the dogmatism of learning, must be finally decided all claim to poetical honours.'[5] This is to put the matter in a different light. 'Common sense' here speaks of a shared, widely accepted, catholic judgement, avoiding eccentricity or exaggeration. This is what John Wesley had in mind. We speak, he says, not in any private language of religious enthusiasm. We use words with a clear, commonly accepted meaning; we speak within the shared universal language of the Christian tradition. We are not founding a new and esoteric sect.

When John Wesley speaks of *common sense* we may see implicit in his words, as in Samuel Johnson's, an appeal not only to the good judgement of his contemporaries, but also to the whole context of Christian discourse through the ages, in which such texts as these need to be seen. Of course the language of absorption, which Charles Wesley does not hesitate to use, needs to be interpreted in the light of the definition of Chalcedon which both John and Charles Wesley wholeheartedly maintained. God and man are united but not confused. They remain distinct even though they are no longer in any way separated. But the mystery which lies at the heart of Christian faith and life involves a union between God and man which is real and awesomely intimate. That also must be underlined. Man is truly called to share not only in what God has, but in what God is.

This very formulation is one which Charles Wesley himself uses. At the end of another of his eucharistic hymns, he prays:

Thy Kingdom come to every heart
And all thou hast, and all thou art.

In another hymn from the same collection he makes the same
assertion and speaks of the active, dynamic union of Christ with
his Church in the self-offering of the *Totus Christus*, the whole
Christ, head and members:

> See where our great High-Priest
>   Before the Lord appears,
> And on his loving breast
>   The tribes of Israel bears,
> Never without his people seen,
> The head of all believing men!
>
> With him, the corner-stone,
>   The living stones conjoin;
> Christ and his Church are one,
>   One body and one vine;
> For us he uses all his powers,
> And all he has, or is, is ours.[6]

Wesley uses a variety of images to describe the union of believers
in and with Christ. Here he speaks of the great High Priest as
carrying our names on his breast. In another place he says they are
graven on his hands as well as on his heart. But the great affirmation
of this hymn is 'Christ and his Church are one'. As Gregory Dix
writes in his description of the Eucharist of the first Christian
centuries:

> the whole church offered the eucharist as the 're-calling' before
> God and man of the offering of Christ. All that which he has
> done once for all as the Priest and Proclaimer of the kingship of
> God, the Church which is 'the fulfilment of him' enters into and
> fulfils. Christ and his Church are one, with one mission, one
> life, one prayer, one gospel, one offering, one being, one Father.[7]

Already almost forty years ago the veteran Methodist scholar
Ernest Rattenbury referred to this passage in his study of Wesley's
eucharistic hymns and pointed to their ecumenical significance.[8] In
the present renewal of eucharistic worship these sacramental hymns
of Charles Wesley could come to play an important part. It is true
that their eighteenth-century style would be a barrier in some places
and for some congregations. But there is in them a potential of
prayer and praise which has never yet been fully realised. They

seem to prophesy the coming of a more united celebration which will unite Catholic and Evangelical in a single act of offering and thanksgiving.

But perhaps the finest of all Charles Wesley's hymns which speak the language of *theosis*, of the change of human into divine nature, is to be found in the section of the *Large Hymn Book* which Wesley headed 'Seeking for full Redemption'. It is a hymn whose Trinitarian structure is clearly evident, in which we see 'the utmost simplicity and plainness' of language at the service of a most profound affirmation of Christian faith:

> Since the Son hath made me free,
> Let me taste my liberty;
> Thee behold with open face,
> Triumph in thy saving grace,
> Thy great will delight to prove,
> Glory in thy perfect love.
>
> Abba, Father, hear thy child,
> Late in Jesus reconciled;
> Hear, and all the graces shower,
> All the joy, and peace, and power,
> All my Saviour asks above,
> All the life and heaven of love.
>
> Heavenly Adam, Life divine,
> Change my nature into thine;
> Move and spread throughout my soul,
> Actuate and fill the whole;
> Be it I no longer now
> Living in the flesh, but thou.
>
> Holy Ghost, no more delay;
> Come, and in thy temple stay;
> Now thine inward witness bear,
> Strong, and permanent and clear;
> Spring of life, thyself impart,
> Rise eternal in my heart.[9]

In one sense the hymn is so translucent as to need no commentary. Yet it may be worthwhile to underline one aspect of its meaning. The whole text celebrates the nowness of eternity. Already, here and now, the Son has set me free. I can triumph through the grace and gift of God. Already I am free to ask with boldness for the whole fulness of the divine life. I can dare to say, 'Heavenly Adam, Life divine, Change my nature into thine.' That all this is turned towards the future, towards an eternal future, is implicit throughout the hymn, as it is explicit in so many of Charles Wesley's other verses. But we can look towards heaven there, only because we already know heaven here. We can look towards sharing the very life of God, because already the Holy Spirit imparts himself to us, the spring of life rises eternally in the very centre of our being.

Such apparently effortless affirmations are not made without great cost. Such insight is not gained without much purification both of heart and mind. I do not speak primarily of the hidden inner work of personal discipleship which lies behind them, though doubtless that is the most important of all. As Rattenbury says, 'Charles Wesley had wept many tears which while they dimmed his sight had clarified his vision.'[10] Rather I refer to the more public, intellectual effort needed to assimilate the given elements of scripture and tradition which such writings presuppose. It goes without saying that the Wesley brothers were rooted and grounded in the Scriptures. But they were also rooted in the subsequent tradition. They loved the early monastic and spiritual writers of the Christian East, as Dr Albert Outler has clearly shown.[11] They loved some of the devotional writers of the Middle Ages. They made full use of the spirituality of the Puritan Movement. They knew that for Christian life and faith to develop it needs the given structures of the doctrines of the creed, the sacraments of the gospel and the traditional practices of Christian discipline, not as techniques which work automatically but as channels, ways by which God's grace may come to us, and we may come to him:

> The prayer, the fast, the word conveys
> When mixed with faith, thy life to me
> In all the channels of thy grace
> I still have fellowship with thee.[12]

So Wesley sings in one of his sacramental hymns, and at once goes on to say that it is chiefly at the table of the Lord that he is fed 'with fulness of immortal bread'.

Furthermore Charles Wesley often based his hymn collections on the theological writings of others. *The Hymns for the Lord's Supper* forms a kind of commentary on a seventeenth-century work of eucharistic theology, *The Christian Sacrament and Sacrifice* of Dr Daniel Brevint. There is a volume of Trinitarian hymns which is based on William Jones of Neyland's classical work, *The Catholic Doctrine of the Holy Trinity*, a notable eighteenth-century statement of the scriptural bases for Trinitarian faith composed as a counterblast to the powerful unitarianising pressures of the time.

Of course as Evangelicals the Wesleys were convinced that all the structures of grace, the 'means' as they called them, were valueless in themselves, taken apart from a living faith in God in Christ. But they also knew that without the structures, the means which God himself has provided, there was no way for the tiny fragment of personal faith and experience which any individual may have received to grow in maturity and balance, to become firm and sure, and thus be rooted in the shared faith and experience of the Christian centuries.[13]

II

We find that this is true when we turn from the Methodist Movement in England to the Methodist Movement in Wales. But here we move from the known to the unknown. Because for the last fourteen hundred years the English have neglected to learn the language of their western neighbours, the English-speaking world as a whole remains in very great ignorance of the content and character of the Welsh tradition. Suffice it to say that eighteenth-century Wales like eighteenth-century England had its Methodist Movement. In Wales as in England the movement began in the 1730s, but though there was frequent contact between the leading figures in the two countries, the two movements developed independently of one another. In Wales the theological tone of the movement was Calvinist and not Arminian; Whitfield had more influence on it than the Wesleys. And in the small world of Welsh-speaking Wales the impact of Methodism on society in general was incomparably greater than it was in England. Much of what has been most characteristic of Welsh Wales during the last two centuries owes its origins to the movement which began in the 1730s.

As in England so also in Wales the movement grew up inside the established Church, and only gradually was forced into schism. In Wales the final break did not occur until 1811, for it was only in that year that the Methodists decided on the step of ordaining their own ministers. The three leaders of the movement in its first generation, Daniel Rowland, Howell Harris and William Williams, Pantycelyn, were respectively an Anglican priest, an Anglican layman and an Anglican deacon. Despite the fact that they received little or no understanding from the episcopate of their time, they were all in different ways reluctant to make any break with the Church, known still in Welsh as *yr hen Fam*, the old Mother.[14]

In the last year of his life, 1790–1, Pantycelyn wrote three long letters, two in Welsh and one in English, to Thomas Charles of

Bala, the young leader of the movement in North Wales and also, be it noted, a clergyman of the Church of England. In them the veteran preacher and writer seems to be handing on a heritage of faith. In the English letter, Pantycelyn looks back over the sixty years of Methodism, and forward to the various dangers which he sees threatening the Methodist societies throughout Wales:

> I hope this Holy Spirit will make you strong against the innumer-able assaults of the Grand Enemy, who continuously tempts to some false and erroneous steps in our most holy religion, some-times to lukewarmness, indifference and indolence on the one hand, as well as to bigotry, enthusiasm and party zeal on the other, and at another time to a loose, irregular, unwatchful life, as well as to pride, self-conceit or false opinions and even heresy on the other. Know my dear brother that heresies now as in the apostles' time, are conceived and brought forth amongst many sects and denominations of people, and boldly preached out without shame or detraction, but as Methodism so far has been kept clear from these pernicious and destructive tares, I hope the Lord will preserve us till the end – and as we have continued now near sixty years orthodox in the faith, I doubt not but we shall spend out our century without erring either in life or doctrine – the Articles of the Church of England, the Nicean and Athanasian Creeds, the lesser and larger catechisms of the assembly with their confession of faith are some of the grandest and most illustrious beauties of the Reformation.[15]

We may perhaps smile to see the Nicene and Athanasian creeds included among the 'illustrious beauties of the Reformation', but the intention of the writer is none the less clear. He values above measure the inheritance of faith which the Methodists have received, an inheritance which explicitly includes the sixteenth-century reaffirmation of the early Christian formulation of the doctrines of the Trinity and the incarnation. To err in these matters for him is to err not only in doctrine but in life. For the Church's teaching about God as Trinity and about the unity of the two natures in the person of our Lord Jesus Christ gives us not bare metaphysical speculations but a vital framework for faith and experience without which the Christian life cannot grow to full maturity and arrive at that wholeness and balance which Pantycelyn sees as so necessary and desirable. Whatever may have been their share in responsibility for the schism which in the end took place, it is clear that men like Pantycelyn did not want to run into sectarianism, but wished to remain in communion with the whole historic Christian tradition of faith and doctrine. Here as in John

Wesley there is implied an appeal to the 'common sense' of the Christian centuries. It is interesting to note that Pantycelyn's second son, John Williams, also a clergyman of the Church of England as well as a Methodist, should in the years immediately after his father's death have translated Jones of Neyland's work on the Holy Trinity into Welsh.[16]

It is important to insist at the outset on these doctrinal concerns in Pantycelyn, because it would be possible to miss their importance in his hymn writing. The theology does not lie so near the surface with him as it does with Charles Wesley. What is immediately apparent is his fervent Christocentric devotion, and his constant celebration of the wonders of the cross. In some ways these are very typical Evangelical hymns. But it is not long before we begin to notice traits which are characteristic of the vision of Pantycelyn and reveal something of his theological interests. He is for instance very much aware of the importance of the doctrine of the incarnation as the necessary presupposition for the doctrine of the atonement. In one place he declares, 'Of all the wonders of heaven this is the greatest, to see the infinite Divine Being wearing the nature of man.'

It is striking too that he sees the work of redemption in various ways. The view of Christ's saving work as one of healing is important for him. In one place in his long poem *Theomemphus* he declares, 'O unfailing, limitless grace, continuing eternally; only in the wounds of the Lamb that died is healing to be found, healing from guilt, healing from fears of the grave, and a love rooted in eternal peace.' Perhaps this thought of Christ as healer is inspired by the close link in Welsh between the words for healing and health, *iachad* and *iechyd*, and the two words used for salvation, *iachawdwriaeth* and *iechydwriaeth*.

Then there is the *Christus victor* theme which recurs in his hymns and which links them with the earlier centuries of Christian doctrine. This has formed the subject of an essay by one of the most distinguished of contemporary Welsh theologians, R. Tudur Jones, in which this point has been powerfully made.[17] In one of his best known verses Pantycelyn affirms: 'I trust in your power, / Great in the work you did once for all. / You conquered death, you conquered hell, / You put down Satan under your feet. / Hill of Calvary, / May this never go from my mind.' We must also notice his remarkable gift of summing up a whole treatise of theology in a single verse:

> In Eden, I shall always remember this,
> I lost blessings without number.
> Down fell my bright crown.

> But the victory of Calvary
> Restored it to me again.
> I shall sing as long as I live.[18]

There is no lack of doctrine here. Pantycelyn did not use the ancient metres and techniques of the Welsh verse; in many ways his style has the same plainness and simplicity which we find in his English contemporaries. But perhaps in this epigrammatic terseness, this capacity to say much in a small constricted space, we catch sight of something which is typical of Celtic poetry through the ages.

As a poet Pantycelyn speaks in images rather than concepts. So it is that we come to recognise in his reference to the fire from heaven, his way of speaking of the coming of the Holy Spirit:

> It is a flame of fire from mid-most heaven
> That has come down into the world,
> Fire that will kindle my stubborn nature,
> Fire that will fill my whole life.
> It will not fail while God remains in being.[19]

This is evidently the fire of the divine love, it is no created reality since it is as eternal as God himself. It is the power and energy of the Holy Spirit which can transform man in his entirety:

> O, a passionate, powerful, strong flame
> Has been enkindled in the heavens.
> It is everlasting love.
> It has made God and myself to be one.[20]

Here it is made explicit that this fire is an everlasting love, a love which is able to unite the believer with God. It is a formulation to which we shall return. Meanwhile we may remark that this fire also has the effect of uniting the believer in himself, of restoring harmony to the different elements of man's nature. In his youth Pantycelyn began training as a medical doctor. He retained throughout his life a keen interest in physical and psychological health, and was particularly renowned as a spiritual counsellor, one who understood the secrets of the heart. His attitudes towards the passions is strikingly positive. The passions are not to be rejected but purified, re-ordered and transformed. 'Nothing but divine grace can restore this order; but it does restore order to the passions, it does not destroy them.' All men's faculties find their fulfilment in God, and in the end in him alone. Neither creation nor man is self-contained, 'a closed box', as Tudur Jones puts it in the essay to which we have already referred.[21]

It would be interesting to investigate in detail how far Pantycelyn was influenced by the seventeenth-century Bishop Edward Reynolds' *Treatise on the Passions and Faculties of the Soul*. It is a work which we know he had in his library and which shows a number of similarities of approach to his own, in its generally affirmative attitude to the passions and its affirmation that it is through the love of God alone that order, proportion and harmony can be restored to the inner life of man. Edward Reynolds' reflection on the likeness of love to fire in particular seems to have caught his attention. 'Love hath', he writes, 'in moral and divine things, the same effect which fire hath in natural – to congregate homogeneal, or things of the same kind, and to separate heterogeneal, or things differing: as we see in the love of God; the deeper the fire, the more is the spiritual part of man collected together and raised from earth.'[22]

Pantycelyn dates from a time before the philosophy of Kant had made its influence felt in Protestant theology, a philosophy which denied that man could have any direct knowledge of the transcendental realm. The fear which haunts so many of our contemporaries that man's mind is not apt for the knowledge of anything beyond this world of space and time does not trouble him. Pantycelyn has no doubt that man can truly know and love God, can enter into a living communion with the Holy Trinity. Indeed he is full of confidence that it is only the knowledge of an eternal transcendent reality which can fill man's heart and mind. Nothing else is an adequate object for man's quest. By his creation in God's image and likeness man was made with an unfulfilled capacity for God. In Christ that fulfilment is beyond anything that man could have conceived. In the Spirit all that is Christ's is imparted to the believer. So in one hymn Pantycelyn prays that God will sanctify his soul 'in every passion and every gift'. And in another he prays:

> Plant in my soul every one
> Of those principles which are like spices
> In your nature;
> Pleasant blossoms which light up earth and heaven.[23]

The virtues which have their origin in God himself, faith, hope, patience, peace, joy, love, are to be planted by God's grace in the very life of man, and are to give beauty and colour to both heaven and earth.

The work of the Holy Spirit is then understood as being to unite man within himself by uniting him with God in a perfect and unbreakable bond, a unity which is founded in the unity of man and God in Christ. The fire of God's love, the power of the Spirit descends into the world, into the heart of man's life and draws out from him a responding movement of love. In one of his English letters, where for a moment we seem to hear in English prose something of the clarity and conciseness which characterises Pantycelyn's poetry in Welsh, he expresses it like this.

> My dear Sister, there is an ocean of happiness prepared for us; and what we experience here is but a drop or a taste of that which we shall enjoy – A sight of his love is the cause of our love; and our thirst after him is but the effect of his thirst after us, and our diligence in seeking of him is the effect of his seeking after us.[24]

As in Charles Wesley, the glimpse of God's glory which we have received draws us on irresistibly to the fulness of vision which shall be.

This is a letter which dates from 1744, the year in which Pantycelyn's first collection of hymns, called simply *Aleluia*, was published. These are the hymns of a young man who sings in the first person singular not so much as an isolated individual but rather as the representative of a whole body of people who have found themselves loved with an everlasting love, who discover that they are heirs to the promises of all the ages. They reflect the first overwhelming sense of the movement that a new day has dawned, that God has come very close to his people in mercy and love and has drawn them into union with himself.[25] So in one of those first hymns Pantycelyn sings:

> He is my fair prince,
> He is my great healer,
> He is my glorious high-priest
> Who continues now to plead.
>
> Good Jesus is my brother,
> My pearl of great price,
> My friend, my gentle love,
> My pure hope,
> My great tree of life,
> My door to go into God,
> My way into the land
> Where my father dwells.
>
> My shining rose of Sharon
> Is Jesus kind and fair,
> My shepherd he, and I
> Am one of his dear flock,

My redeemer without fail,
My bridegroom unconcealed,
My strong shield, my good guide,
My sure lot and seal.

Great Alpha and Omega is he,
The dear Christ is my right,
He is my quiet refuge,
He is my faithful witness,
My head, my horn, my tower,
My pure, golden altar,
My precious sacrifice, my great prophet
Who leads me ever on.[26]

The piling up of images seeks to express the amazed sense of intimacy, of identification with Christ Jesus. The accumulation of biblical titles for the Lord, some familiar, some less so, speak of a Christological interpretation of scripture, or better of a Christo-logical assimilation of scripture. As Pantycelyn says of one of his spiritual heroes, 'he becomes one with the whole Bible, one with all the faithful throughout the world, one with the Law of Sinai; one with the free promise'.[27] The whole history of salvation belongs to each believer. Our personal history becomes part of the universal history of God's presence with his people.

There is in Pantycelyn's writing often a sense of great immediacy. The hymns are written for the most part in simple and apparently unstudied language. There are roughnesses of vocabulary and grammar which have pained the scholars of Wales. But at the same time we feel that we are being carried forward on the wings of the Spirit. 'There is no suggestion that here or elsewhere he deliberately hunted through Scripture for embellishments. What has happened, more significantly, is that his own way of apprehending the world has been modified by the intensity of his imaginative experience of the Old Testament and the Book of Revelation. The language is scriptural because the imagery is lived Scripture.'[28] The Spirit which breathed in the original writers breathes in the eighteenth-century preacher as he sits in his South Wales farmhouse; his consciousness is changed.

It is significant that among the books of the Bible which Pantycelyn particularly commends to the Christian hymn writer is the Song of Songs. The traditional interpretation of that book as speaking of the love of God for his creation, for his Church and for every member of the Church, has its origins in the earliest Christian centuries. It is one of the things which unites the fathers of the Church with the great writers of the western Middle Ages,

St Bernard above all, and with the Puritan preachers and teachers of the seventeenth century. Pantycelyn has all this history behind him, and in his hands the theme is taken up again into a new celebration of God's love for his people, and a new vision of his transcendent majesty and beauty; he sings first of the beauty of the divine plan revealed in the birth and death of the Saviour, and then he sings of the beauty of God himself beyond all the imaginings of men.

> Your beauty will be forever new
>   Forever freshly kindling a fire
> Through all the ages of eternity
>   Without ever coming to an end.
> A fervent flame, without ending,
>   Through all the ranks of heaven,
> It will continue to burn brightly
>   As long as God himself shall last. [29]

This is a beauty which captures man's mind as well as his heart, which awakens in him thoughts which are beyond thought. It is a transforming beauty which can change man's whole being. We notice again the image of the fire which is no less eternal than God himself.

> If here and now the beauty of your face
>   Causes myriads to love you,
> What will your glad beauty do
>   There in the expanses of eternity?
> The Heaven of heavens
>   Will marvel at you ceaselessly for ever.
>
> What height will my love reach then
>   What wonder will be mine,
> When I shall see your glory
>   Perfect and full on Mount Sion?
>   Infinity
> Of all beauties gathered into one.
>
> What thoughts above understanding
>   Shall I find there within myself
> When I see that the Godhead
>   Perfect and pure, and I are one?
> There is a bond
>   Which there is no language able to express.
>
> The bond was made in eternity,

It is sure, strong, great in power
Millions of ages
Cannot break it or undo it,
    It abides and will abide
As long as God himself shall last.

This hymn comes from the collection of 1762, *Farewell Visible, Welcome Invisible Things*, and the verses have a majestic quality to them, as well as a transparent simplicity. We are dealing here with the mature Pantycelyn in the fulness of his power. As Saunders Lewis remarks, in these hymns Williams begins to speak in a more philosophical fashion: 'In this period the newest thing in his style is this philosophical element, and its function is more and more to purify his love, to give it a vision which is more and more divine, to change his life itself into a symbol of the possibility of human nature.' When human love arrives at the being of God it is transformed into a pure contemplative joy, 'pure vision untroubled by desire, the highest state to which the person can attain'. This is joy at the fact that God is in himself the fulness of all being. 'Your perfect being is my joy,' Pantycelyn declares.[30] In this movement both the heart and the mind are drawn out beyond themselves into a transforming union with God through this vision of divine beauty, in which all lesser beauties are gathered into one. We observe that for Pantycelyn as for Hooker it is faith which perceives God as truth, while it is love which grasps God as beauty. But the truth which the believing mind perceives, the thought beyond understanding which he there finds within himself, is that I, in all the fragility, sinfulness, mortality of my nature, have been made one with the pure and perfect Godhead. This is the union, the bond, which there is no language able to express.

The Welsh word translated 'bond' is *cwlwm*. It is a very concrete word. It can be used of many kinds of knot, or of an intricate design in art or in music. It can be used of the marriage bond. It is a union which is indissoluble. Pantycelyn goes on to tell us more of this in the next two verses:

The bonds of nature will all be broken,
    Its laws will go for nothing:
But my union with the heavens
    Is of much greater power:
        It is unchanging
    Exactly as my God is.

Neither life nor death
    Nor the greatest of the angels

> Neither cherubim, nor powers
> > Nor all the hosts of heaven above
> Can separate me
> > For all eternity from his love.[31]

Pantycelyn takes up the great Pauline words 'What can separate us from the love of God in Christ Jesus?' and interprets them in terms of the union established between God and man in the incarnation of the Word. In Christ we see the true destiny of every human being. The bond which links man to eternity is immeasurably more powerful than all the bonds which bind him to earth, for he was made for God and can only find himself in God. And the bond which unites man with God is itself divine, unchangeable, exactly as God is unchangeable. In terms of classical Christian theology our union with God is made possible because both the Son and the Spirit are of one substance (*homo-ousios*) with the Father. We are united with the Father in the Son who at once is both man and God through the power of the Spirit who is also truly God, and who makes us participant in God. He is the joy and the beauty of the Father and the Son, a joy and a beauty which overflow into the world and carry man up into the Trinitarian exchange of love.

It is very important to recognise the Trinitarian goal to which all Pantycelyn's language about love for the divine beauty tends. It is the eternal glory of the Triune God which is the ultimate object of man's longing and man's love, and this is a human love which is already penetrated through and through with the divine love. This love for God as he is in himself reflects back on and transfigures all truly human loving, in particular the love which the believer feels for the humanity of Jesus, his Saviour and his Lord. This is the context in which we need to read Pantycelyn's verses which speak of his love for the Son of Mary. They are often of great intensity and they frequently make use of the imagery of the Song of Songs. But this human love is always supported by and transfigured by the love which comes from God himself. It is called out by the beauty of the divine compassion which shines out in the cross, above all in the wounds of the Saviour which bring our healing. Through this narrow point in space, the hill of Calvary, through this narrow point in time, 'one afternoon', as Pantycelyn loves to say, all God's love is poured out into the world and all man's love is carried up into the vision of God's eternal beauty, the beauty of the sacrificial love which lies at the heart of the Godhead. As Ralph Cudworth had put it, 'The Gospel is nothing else but God, descending into the world in our form and conversing with us in our likeness that he might allure and draw us up to God and make us partakers of his divine form.'[32]

There is in all this one ascending movement of man's heart and mind, called out in response to the descent of God's love into the world. In this process the reality of human loving is neither negated nor despised. Pantycelyn knows much about it and can write of it with balance and perception at the appropriate time. But here in man's approach to God, even more than in man's approach to his fellow men, what is merely human needs for its fulfilment what is more than human. Man's being and man's love are made in order to go beyond themselves into the divine being and the divine love. Man was created for a joy greater than earthly joy, for a beauty which is transcendent and eternal. Without it his nature is starved and stunted. When here and now it is even glimpsed, then at once his existence begins to take on the dimensions of eternity.

We have come to see again in a different context how it is that the doctrines of Trinity, incarnation and deification belong together in an indissoluble knot. Self-giving love is at the very heart of God; the love with which the Father loves the Son, in which the Spirit joys, is a love before all time. From all eternity in the council of the Three in One man's salvation was foreseen. And in that love we are all included, sons in the Son, made alive in the Spirit with the very life of God. This faith which in visual form is wonderfully expressed in one of the greatest Russian icons, Rublev's icon of the Holy Trinity, finds memorable expression in a different medium in many of the hymns of Welsh Methodism. It is one of their favourite themes of wonder and praise.

But this mystery of eternal love is not only at the root of all things, it is also at their consummation. It is the substance of the vision of heaven which captures the heart and mind of the man or woman of faith. And what was in the beginning and what shall be in the end is, in part, made present and made known, here in the meanwhile in this world of space and time, of alienation and death. It is made known especially in the Church's worship and above all at its heart in the sacrament of the divine love, the Holy Communion.

III

There is only one other of the many hymn writers of Welsh Methodism whom we can begin to compare with Pantycelyn, and that is Ann Griffiths (1776–1805). It speaks much for the transcendent quality of her vision that it does not seem inappropriate to place the handful of hymns she has left us beside the massive corpus of Pantycelyn's work. Even more than he, she was one who penetrated into the wonders of the divine being and was lost in their glory, one in whom love human and love divine were fused together in a white heat of pure desire. There is one verse of hers, which, it is said, she composed as she rode back over the Berwyn hills from Bala on a Sunday when she had been to Communion, which sums this up in unforgettable words:

> O blessed hour of eternal rest
>> From my labour, in my lot,
> In the midst of a sea of wonders
>> With never a sight of an end or a shore;
> Abundant freedom of entrance, ever to continue,
>> Into the dwelling places of the Three in One.
> Water to swim in, not to be passed through,
>> Man as God, and God as man.[33]

Ann is a writer of extreme precision. She does not say, as some commentators have suggested, that she is simply absorbed into the sea of the divine being. She rejoices at it in a wonder which will never cease. Human nature is not confused or simply merged with the divine in such a way as to be annihilated. But it is united with it in a union without separation. The last line of the verse has in Welsh a stronger meaning than can easily appear in English. The word *yn*, which is rendered *as*, might also be translated by the word *being*, man being God, God being man. Before the mystery we may well fall silent. We can only be astonished at the way the ancient theme of man's participation in God finds such expression in the eighteenth century alike in Welsh and English Methodism.

In recent years a new factor has emerged in our theological world through the appearance of the first volumes of the English translation of von Balthasar's great work, *Herrlichkeit*, this sustained and monumental effort to restore the idea of beauty to its place alongside truth and goodness in our approach to the things of God. It is a book which gives rise to a renewed evaluation of the whole contemplative element within the Christian tradition, not only in the profound but very specific form which we find in the great Carmelites of sixteenth-century Spain but also in its earlier and more varied forms in Christian East and West alike, in Gregory of Nyssa and Augustine, for instance, in Bernard and Symeon the New Theologian, in Bonaventure and Gregory Palamas. This element is clearly central in Orthodoxy and Catholicism, but has it any place in the world of the Reformation?

In the light of the last two chapters it is surely possible to give a more positive answer to this question than von Balthasar seems ready to allow. Can we fail to recognise Hooker and Andrewes, Charles Wesley and Pantycelyn as contemplatives in this older, less closely defined but more theological sense of the word? For us the answer seems self-evident, and von Balthasar's work with its amazingly wide erudition sheds much light on the interpretation of texts such as those which we have been considering. His wide-ranging historical study of the Christian tradition provides the kind of context which is needed for their full appreciation. He shows us much about the structure of their *ecstatic* experience and how it can be understood. For it is only as we are being taken out of ourselves into the life of God that we can even begin to enter into an understanding of the things of God:

> In theology there are no 'bare facts' which, in the name of an alleged objectivity of detachment, disinterestedness and impar- tiality, one could establish like any other worldly facts, without oneself being (both objectively and subjectively) grasped so as to participate in the divine nature (*participatio divinae naturae*). For the object with which we are concerned is man's participation in God, which from God's perspective is actualised as 'revelation' (culminating in Christ's Godmanhood) and which from man's perspective is actualised as 'faith' (culminating in participation in Christ's Godmanhood). This double and reciprocal *ekstasis* – God's 'venturing forth' to man and man's to God – constitutes the very content of dogmatics, which may then rightly be presented as a theory of rapture; the *admirabile commercium et connubium* between God and man in Christ as Head and Body.[34]

If this is indeed the case, as I should maintain in unison with von Balthasar, then we must say that the hymns we have been looking at are indeed dogmatic as well as liturgical texts. They bear witness to just this double reciprocal *ekstasis* of God to man and man to God. They testify to the Church's faith in God as Trinity of love, into whose life we are called to enter. They see our human nature, despite all the ravages of sin, as made with a capacity to enter into that unity of life which is in God himself, to share in the divine nature. Even texts which are so familiar as to be dulled almost beyond recognition reveal something of their original meaning when placed in this context. It is so with the most familiar of all Charles Wesley's hymns which speaks of this divine love, this joy of heaven which comes down to earth and fixes his dwelling among us, so that receiving the fulness of grace we may serve God with all the angelic hosts in a life of unceasing prayer and praise, which leads us from glory to glory till we find our place in the kingdom of heaven, lost in wonder, love and praise.

A Life which is both His and Theirs:
E. B. Pusey and the Oxford Movement

The Methodist and Evangelical movements, which were considered in Chapter 3, spread right across the Reformation world in Europe and North America. They began in one of those moments when simultaneously, but without any apparent connection, men and women in a variety of places are stirred into new vision and new life. There was no one controlling centre of the revival. The situation was different in the movement of Catholic renewal which began a century later in the thirties of the nineteenth century. Here, though by no means confined to Oxford, it was focused there in a remarkable way. For the ten years which followed 1833 the old university city saw an extraordinary ferment of prayer and life, of thought and action. It was a ferment which centred on three men who for most of this time were very closely united in a common endeavour: John Keble, Edward Bouverie Pusey and John Henry Newman. The movement reached a decisive turning point in 1845 with Newman's conversion to Roman Catholicism. That event did not bring the movement to a close in the churches in communion with Canterbury. It some ways it made it go deeper and spread its influence more widely. But the first most creative and exuberant phase of the movement was over.

Recent years have seen a renewed interest in the history of the Oxford Movement and a growing conviction among at least some commentators that the years from 1833 to 1845 do not constitute a totally closed episode in the past. Rather they are seen as years in which something of lasting and universal significance was disclosed, something whose meaning is perhaps only becoming fully evident now. The Oxford Movement has left us with much unfinished business. There are aspects of what happened then which have never been fully understood, which it remains for us to elucidate and appropriate. This is clearly true of the ecumenical dimensions of the movement, and of its prophetic role in reopening the broken dialogue between Rome and the Reformation. Only since the Second Vatican Council has it been possible to see the positive significance of Newman's conversion, an act which was not merely personal, but which in a strange way brought the churches together by taking from one to the other a man who carried with him all that was best in the tradition in which he had developed and matured. Pusey alone in 1845 saw this positive meaning in Newman's move, and thirty years ago it was still difficult to see in Pusey's words about Newman's action more than the wishful thinking of one who refused to face all the consequences of the parting of the ways. Seen from our present vantage point we can recognise in Pusey's judgement a depth of insight which others lacked. Beyond the sorrow of the separation he saw the possibility of new life and understanding brought about by Newman's obedience to the will of God.[1]

I

No less central to the concerns of the Oxford Movement is the subject of this book, the reaffirmation of the doctrine of *theosis*, seen as an immediate consequence of the doctrine of the incarnation, and the foundation of a new and transformed vision of the calling and destiny of man. For man is lifted up into participation in God by the loving movement of God's coming to share in the very nature and predicament of man. Here again the ecumenical consequences of this affirmation were to be incalculable. This doctrine, which was at the heart of the Christianity of East and West in the first millennium of the Christian era, and which has remained central in the Christianity of the Orthodox East, suddenly came to new life with unexpected power in the middle of nineteenth-century England. It was as if there were a veritable epiphany of patristic spirituality and theology in the midst of our divided western Christendom, an epiphany which would draw together into new possibilities of reconciliation elements of the Reformation heritage and elements of the continuing tradition of the churches in communion with Rome. Here again there is much unfinished business, much in the original vision of the Oxford Movement which has not yet been realised and appropriated.

One thing is clear. The Oxford Movement combined in a remarkable way a rediscovery of doctrine with a renewal of life, a search for the fulness of the faith which was at the same time a search for a life of holiness. In this movement there was no separation between theology and spirituality, between theory and practice. Everything that was seen of the will of God made an immediate demand on man's obedience. As an eminent French authority on this subject wrote some thirty years ago in a study of Newman:

The most powerful and also the most respectable attraction of the new movement was to put forward and multiply examples of a Christianity which was at one and the same time eager for holiness and creative of it. It was the demands which this religion made, not simply in abstract, but immediately and in practice, which gained for it such enthusiastic and effective support. The greatness of the Tractarian movement was that it was neither a simply intellectual revival, nor . . . a religious revival without doctrinal basis. The theological effort carried a spiritual renewal inescapably with it, while the most genuine religious needs lay at the root of its speculative researches.

Among the great Tractarians, this truth took flesh in a way which one can only describe as resplendent and which makes this group of men the honour not only of England but of the whole of Christendom of the last century. They carried on their work, moved by the one only desire to give unconditional obedience to the will of God proclaimed in Christ Jesus. Their particular merit was that they recognised with a clarity which was specially remarkable in the middle of the romantic period that there can be no Christian holiness save that which is founded on truth.[2]

What Bouyer remarks on here is the unity of intellectual and spiritual excellence, the fusion of practical and theoretical concerns which marked the beginnings of the movement. After 1845 it was for some time the practical and pastoral element which predominated. The Oxford Movement marked the beginning of a growth in life, liturgy and devotion in the churches of the Anglican communion which is still continuing. From these years came the renewal of sacramental worship which has brought the Eucharist back into the centre of the life of Anglican congregations right across the world. It had not been so in the eighteenth century. John and Charles Wesley were not at all typical in their practice of frequent Communion. From this time there dates a new ideal of pastoral practice, which sent clergy into the most deprived of the inner city areas of Victorian England and out on to the new frontier of the mid-West in America, and opened up a new vision of what a sacrificial priestly ministry could mean. From these years we date the beginnings of the recovery of religious and monastic life in the churches of the Anglican communion. The first of the communities of sisters was founded in 1845, the very year of Newman's departure. All these developments were marked by a longing for holiness, and for the fulness of Catholic truth. They were also marked by a longing for unity. All of them in different ways were inspired by the teaching, preaching and example of the three men who stood at the movement's heart, Pusey, Keble and Newman.

I link the three names deliberately, because in recent years Newman has received so much more attention than his two companions that it is easy to miss the extent to which in these years they were working, thinking, praying and planning together. Newman was certainly the most brilliant of them. He had a creative theological and philosophical mind, and a magnificent English prose style which neither Keble nor Pusey could match. But Pusey was, in Newman's own judgement, a man of more massive erudition than himself, a man of a large independent mind, and a powerful and passionate preacher. Keble, the eldest of the three, in some ways the originator of the whole movement, had a more subtle and penetrating intellect than his modesty allowed him easily to reveal. The re-reading of his writings from this period has surprised some students who expected to find only the gentle author of devotional verse.

For all of them this doctrine that we are called to share in the divine nature became increasingly important as the movement developed. Andrew Louth has spoken of this well in an essay which points to the interconnections of the doctrines of the incarnation, deification and the Trinity. He shows how Newman in his *Lectures on Justification*, published in 1836, 'expresses this central conviction of the Oxford Movement, the conviction that as we respond to God in Christ, God himself is present to us, in our hearts, drawing us to himself; a conviction which expresses the heart of the patristic doctrine of deification'.[3] In these *Lectures*, in Bouyer's view Newman's most important and creative theological work in this period, Newman argues that the Reformers were right in insisting that our justification is wholly the work of Christ. They were wrong in teaching that this righteousness is only imputed to us and not imparted. Christ himself becomes our righteousness. 'Our true righteousness is the indwelling of our glorified Lord . . . This is to be justified, to receive the Divine Presence with us and to be made a Temple of the Holy Ghost.' So Newman can affirm 'justification comes *through* the sacraments; is received by faith; *consists* in God's inwards presence; and *lives* in obedience'. This understanding of justification has immediate ethical implications. It makes demands on the believer which we can only with difficulty meet. 'Such an inhabitation (of the Spirit) brings the Christian into a state altogether new and marvellous . . . and gives him a place and office which he had not before . . . In St Peter's forcible language he becomes "partaker of the Divine Nature", and has power or authority as St John says "to become son of God".'[4]

If Newman sees the doctrine of our participation in the divine nature as a key to resolving some of the most profound Reformation controversies, Keble sees it as a way in which we may come to understand the whole purpose of God in creation and redemption. In a note to a poem written for the second Sunday after Epiphany, which meditates on the story of Cana in Galilee, Keble writes:

The change of water into wine was believed by the ancients to typify the change which St Paul in particular so earnestly dwells on, 'Old things are become new', and St John, 'He that sitteth upon the Throne saith, Behold I make all things new.' Accordingly St Cyprian applies the first miracle to the admission of the Gentiles into the Church. And St Augustine to the Evangelical interpretation of the Old Testament. And St Cyril of Alexandria to the Spirit superseding the letter. This then the beginning of miracles, a kind of pattern for the rest, showed how Christ's glory was to be revealed in the effects of his sacramental touch; whether immediately, as when he touched the leper and healed him, or through the hem of his garment, or by the saints, his living members, according to his promise, 'The works that I do, ye shall do also; and greater works than these shall ye do, because I go to my Father.' Thus according to the Scriptures, the sacramental touch of the Church is the touch of Christ, and her system is '*deifica disciplina*', a rule which, in some sense, makes men gods and the human divine; and all this depends on the verity of the incarnation, therefore his mother is especially instrumental in it, besides being, as nearest to him, the most glorious instance of it. 'The Mother of Jesus is there, and both Jesus and his disciples are called' (He as Bridegroom and author of the whole mystery, they as ministers, servants and instruments) to the mysterious 'marriage' or communion of saints.[5]

These thoughts were not passing fancies. Some twenty years later, in the last years of his life, preaching to students preparing for the ministry at Cuddesdon, Keble could say:

Christ is come, not indeed in the Body, but by a nearer, far nearer Presence – by his Spirit; not only *with* them but *within* them. In Him they now live a new life, which they have entirely from him, a life which is both His and theirs, whereby they are so joined to him as to be verily and indeed partakers of a divine nature. Yes, brethren, this and no less was the mysterious Whitsun privilege and glory of those on whom the Holy Ghost first came down; a glory so high and inconceivable that the Holy

Fathers did not hesitate to call it deification, and Christianity which teaches and confesses it, they called a 'deifying discipline'.[6]

We notice here how the theology of Newman's *Lectures on Justification* finds crystalline expression in the preaching of Keble. We see his love for the phrase 'a deifying discipline', *deifica disciplina*. It is a phrase which speaks of a way of loving discipleship, a way of attention and obedience, of learning and constant practice in 'The trivial round, the common task' of life. Forty years earlier in one of the most familiar of the hymns in *The Christian Year* he had taught that it was in such things that we were to find a way which would 'bring us daily nearer God', and enable us to find God's presence in and through all things. What he taught, he lived. So as he walked about his country parish in Hampshire he would pray, 'Lord who hast given me eyes to see/ and love this sight so fair,/ give me a heart to seek out thee,/ and find thee everywhere.'[7]

II

Having looked briefly at the teaching of Keble and Newman on this subject, we come now to look a little more closely at the position of E. B. Pusey. From all Pusey's writings I intend to take a single volume of sermons, those preached in the week following the consecration of St Saviour's Church in Leeds in October 1845.[8] It is true to say that Pusey's writings have been shamefully neglected by Anglicans in this century. Nowhere is this clearer than in this particular set of sermons which reveal Pusey's spiritual theology at its deepest and most powerful. They were sermons preached in very particular circumstances at a critical moment in the history of the Oxford Movement. Newman had just gone to Rome. What reaction were his friends to make? Was there to be a renewal of the old traditional anti-Roman polemic? There were many who wished that there should be. Even some of those close to Pusey hoped he would demonstrate his loyalty to the Church of England by denouncing the conduct of his former colleague. There is, as we shall see, not a trace of such denunciation in these sermons. Their whole tone is eirenic in the extreme, both towards Rome and towards the Evangelicals. One sermon is directed specifically to what we may call a programme for spiritual ecumenism. They showed a new way forward, a way from which we can still learn much.

But there was a more personal and particular side to the circumstances of this consecration, which also had its part in giving a special tone of intensity and authenticity to Pusey's preaching here. The new church which had been consecrated was built in a deprived inner city area. It was built – though no one at the time knew this – entirely at Pusey's expense, in memory of his dearly loved daughter Lucy and as a sign of his own deepening penitence. Pusey had had to face every kind of difficulty and disappointment in the actual construction of the church, particularly in his relations with the bishop of the diocese, who suspected his every move, and saw threats of popery in every detail of the building. Of all this Pusey says nothing in his sermons. He simply takes them as a God-given occasion to reaffirm the faith of the Church as he has come to understand it.

If then the tone of these sermons is consistently eirenic, one cannot say that it is always serene. There is, on the one side, a darkness, an austerity and a rigour when he speaks of the dangers of eternal loss, which may trouble us. But on the other side there is a tone of ecstatic joy when he comes to speak of the end of the Christian life, our union with God in heaven, a joy which may also disturb us, though in a different way. Many years ago the Swedish scholar, Yngve Brilioth spoke of Pusey as the *doctor mysticus* of the Oxford Movement. In the light of these sermons the title does not seem inappropriate.

As always in his preaching so here Pusey constantly quotes from scripture and the fathers. He is aware that he is putting before his congregation a very high and demanding doctrine which is unfamiliar to them. He had already been denounced and inhibited from preaching in the University of Oxford for precisely this reason. So he seeks to show at every step that his teaching is not his own, but that of the Church through the ages, and in particular of the Church in the first five centuries to which Anglicans had always since the Reformation made special appeal. But he does not restrict himself to that early period. The tradition did not cease then. And so Pusey cites at length some of the great writers of the Middle Ages, Anselm, Bernard, Ruysbroeck to show the consonance of his teaching with that of his fathers in the faith. This doctrine, he tells us, is not his own in the sense that it is some private individual discovery, some esoteric experience with which he seeks to surprise the world. What he proclaims is the common, universal experience of the saints. But that he has made this teaching his own in the depths and the heights of his own experience is equally clear from these sermons. They are not simply the product of book-learning. The painful experiences of self-reproach, the agonised depths of penitence through which he passed in this decade, are surely only the other side of the brilliance of the vision of the divine glory which shines out in these pages. The great saints are full of what seem to us exaggerated acknowledgements of their sin. The light and clarity of God which they have glimpsed show up the distress and misery of man in ways which are unfamiliar to us.

We have said that Pusey is concerned in these sermons with the question of Christian unity. This is particularly the case in the last but one of the sermons.[9] Its theme is the ancient one that our only perfection in this life is to know our imperfection, and so always to press onwards towards the fulness to which God calls us. We must hold fast to what we already have and press on from there. This is true in the affairs of every day. It is particularly true in the perplexing situation of the divided churches. This is the one sermon in which Pusey quotes Newman directly, and it is instructive to see what he quotes and the context in which he quotes it.

> Yes! my brethren, wherever we are in the Christian course, as we have all one End, God; one Faith, in the One Object of Faith, the Everblessed, Coequal, Coeternal Trinity, as that faith has been revealed to us and fenced round against every error in our Creed; one Hope, to see Him; one food of life, himself in his sacraments; one Spirit, who is the life of all the members of the one body, the life of all alike, although his gifts be manifold; – so also for saints as for penitents, there is only one way to Heaven, to walk on in him who is the way, to hold fast that ye have and press onward. This is the remedy of all doubts in faith and practice. 'One step' it has been well said, 'enough for me'. Today is thine, by the gift of God; tomorrow as yet is his. Fear not whither you may be led; see only that you be now 'led by the Spirit of God'; led, not going before, not holding back, not standing still, but led.' It is the very part of faith, to go forth as Abraham went, not knowing whither he went.[10]

Into this way of unity, Pusey believes, we shall be led if we are willing to let ourselves be taught by the prayers we say, the hymns we sing, the sacraments we celebrate. If we are to go forward we need to live by the spirit of the liturgy.

> Would that we living in a Church founded by God, could all so live, day by day, in the devotions, creeds, hymns of praise preserved to us in her, as to imbibe their spirit in ourselves. This would be no uncertain voice to us, did we learn it in the presence and the house of God. Words have a different meaning when tossed to and fro in argument, and when prayed in the communion of saints, the voice of the one Dove, moaning to her Lord. The full heart then stints not the meaning of the words; thinks not how little they may mean, but how much; a ray of

light falls upon them from above; we stand not without them, as judges, but within them as worshippers; he who has taught the Church her prayers is present in our souls; and with his blessed unction from above, 'Comfort, Life and Fire of Love' anoints both them and us. Disputing divides, devotion knits in one; for in it we pray to one, through one, by one.[11]

It is one of the characteristics of the leaders of the Oxford Movement that they had a sharp awareness of how much the meaning of words depends on the context in which they are placed and on the person who uses them. Keble, for instance, has remarkable things to say on this subject in his Tract on the patristic interpretation of the Scriptures. Words which are banal and empty in the mouth of one – 'God is love', for instance – acquire the force of a dazzling revelation when they are spoken by one whose life has been shaped by them. As a contemporary Japanese theologian, the Jesuit Fr Kadowaki puts it, 'Nothing touches our hearts more than the words of someone who has actually experienced what he is talking about.'[12] These are words which in some sense have become what they signify in the life of the one who uses them. As a Syriac writer of the seventh century puts it, speaking of prayer: 'When you recite the words of the prayer . . . be careful not just to repeat them but let yourself *become* these words. For there is no advantage in reciting them unless the word actually becomes embodied in you and becomes a deed, with the result that you are seen in the world to be a man of God.'[13] Such an embodiment of prayer in flesh and blood is the work of the Holy Spirit in the one who prays, a work of transformation and union with God, in which the words become the vehicle of divine grace and power. Thus words which have become shallow and hard through their use in controversy become supple and full of meaning when used in prayer and meditation. They begin again to fulfil the healing and unifying function for which they were originally intended. They become active and effective. So, for instance, the familiar words of the Psalms acquire a new power when we hear them in the choir of a monastic community. They are charged with the depth of silence from which they come, a silence in which the Spirit is present and at work. The many levels of meaning implicit in the sacred text begin to unfold themselves through the action of the divine grace which is itself both manifold and one.

As Pusey observes here, when we stand outside the words of faith and worship, as judges, we fail to understand them. When we enter into these words as worshippers we discover their true meaning and purpose. We see further when we kneel. The Holy Spirit descends on us and on them; there is a double *epiclesis* or invocation. Through them he brings us into union with one another in God and with God in one another. Here is the basis for a whole programme of spiritual ecumenism, as we learn to worship with those from whom we have been separated. Here, above all others, is the way which will help us to enter into the hearts and minds of our separated brethren, which will lead us to mutual confession and forgiveness, where we have wronged one another. There is thus, for instance, no better way for any western Christian of coming to understand Eastern Orthodoxy than to learn to pray in the divine liturgy. But here too is a principle which is true, *mutatis mutandis*, in a different and wider realm. In the work of dialogue between the religions it is those who have been willing to share the silence and the prayer of the others who have brought most insight and understanding to this question, a Thomas Merton, a William Johnston, a Jules Monchanin, a Louis Massignon. Here is the way in which Pusey himself came to live within the words of scripture and the fathers, dwelling on them, dwelling in them, not so much assimilating them as letting himself be assimilated by them. Hence it was that he seemed to be wholly within his utterances. 'Pusey seemed to inhabit his sentences,' wrote J. B. Mozley. It was this which gave his preaching such power.[14]

Let us then turn to hear him speak directly on our subject of man's call to share in the nature of God, to enter into the communion of the divine life. Here we are quoting from Sermon XV, on 'The Bliss of Heaven', preached on the text 1 John 3:2.

'Know ye not, he saith, that ye are the temple of God, and that the Spirit of God dwelleth in you?' Not through any creature could we be made partakers of God; not angel or arch-angel could dwell in the soul, but God alone who made it for himself. 'So, says a Father [Cyril of Alexandria], have we the rich gift that he who is by nature and truly God is our indweller and inhabitant, in that from the Father we receive the Spirit who is both from him and in him, and his own being, by name and truth, equally Lord with himself, and to us replacing the Son, as being of one nature with him.' 'Christ sent to us the Comforter from heaven, through whom and with whom, he is with us and dwelleth in us, pouring into us no foreign but his own Spirit, of his own substance and that of his Father.' And so our blessed Lord says again, 'If any man love me, he will keep my words and my Father will love him, and we will come unto him and make our abode with him.' And lest anyone think that the Father and the Son only, without the Holy Spirit make their abode with those who love him, let him consider what was said just before of the Holy Spirit 'whom the world cannot receive, because it seeth him not, neither knoweth him, but ye know him, for he dwelleth with you and shall be in you'.[15]

So, weightily, technically almost does Pusey set out his faith in the words of the fourth Evangelist and of the partriarch of Alexandria. But then he bursts out in his own words:

O the depth of the riches of the condescension and love of God, who hath not only pardoned us and delivered us from death, but given us righteousness and sanctification; not given them us only, but as Scripture says, himself made his Son such to us, by taking our nature into God, and in our nature dying for us; and not only so, but imparting his grace; and not grace only, but making us sons; and not sons only, but members of his only-begotten Son; not heirs only, but co-heirs with Christ; to have in our measure, what he has, the everlasting love of the everlasting Father; and of this he hath given us the earnest, his Holy Spirit, who with him is one God, to dwell in us, in his own holy person and unite us with him.[16]

From this reappropriation of the patristic understanding of the indwelling of God in man there flow many consequences, practical and theoretical, for our understanding of our human nature and of our calling towards both God and our fellow-man. There is in man an openness towards self-transcendence both in love and in knowledge which takes many forms. There is, for instance, a new awareness of the fact that while God's love for each one is personal and unique, a thing on which the Evangelicals had greatly insisted, it is never merely individual as opposed to personal. There is in these sermons a wonderful restatement of the co-inherence of each in all and of all in each, which is one facet of Pusey's whole vision of God in man and man in God. In speaking of the joy of God over the sinner who repents, for instance, Pusey says God's joy:

is not only over our whole redeemed race; it is, Holy Scripture says, in all its fulness over each single penitent sinner. Holy Scripture speaks of all as one, since all, though many, are one body in Christ; and yet again, all which is true of the whole, is true of each single living member, so that each member may in the Psalms or Canticles or the Song of Songs, as being in the body, take the words of the body. For God's love, being infinite, is bounded not in itself, but by our power to receive it; whom he loveth, he loveth infinitely, for his is an infinite love. As we are taught to say to God in the words of the psalmist, 'O God, thou art *my* God,' though he is the God of all, visible and invisible; so of God our Redeemer, St Paul saith, 'I live by the faith of the Son of God, who loved *me* and gave himself for me.' 'The measure of his love to each' sayeth a holy father [Chrysostom] 'is as great as the whole world', so that we might boldly say, 'So boundless was his love, that he would not have grudged his sufferings though but for one'; 'The joy which he hath in the redemption of the world, he hath in the conversion of a single soul, and we owe as deep a debt of love, as though he had came for us alone'; yea deeper far since the salvation of others is our gain, not his; for the bliss of all shall increase the bliss of each, while each in each beholds the glory of God reflected and in the glory of each shall we have our own special joy.[17]

These words, which speak of the presence of the whole Church in each of its members, recapitulate the traditional Christian teaching about the meaning of the solitary life, in which something of the unbounded possibilities of each human person, made in God's image and likeness, is revealed. This teaching finds classical expression in the West in 'The Book of the Lord be with you' by St Peter Damian. In this treatise there is a discussion of the nature of the prayer which is made by hermits, those who though physically alone are not alone in the Spirit. Because each person contains the whole within himself, St Peter argues, the one who lives in solitude may rightly make use of the liturgy which belongs to the whole Church. By his very existence the hermit reveals in himself the unity of the Church and the catholicity of the human person. Such teaching was far from being merely a matter of abstract speculation or historical research for Pusey and those who learnt from him. One of the very first Sisters of the Society of the Holy Trinity at Ascot, the religious community with which Pusey was most closely connected, lived for many years as a recluse within the buildings of the community. At the time when this sermon was preached in 1845 Sister Clara (Clarissa Powell) was already under Pusey's spiritual direction. Two years later she entered the community. From 1851 onwards she began for periods to live a life of greater silence and solitude. She remained throughout her life in close contact with Pusey. One of the last letters he wrote, less than a month before his death in 1882, is addressed to her. Its words reveal something of the human content of this theological vision of our capacity for love, human and divine, a vision which had been worked out in long years of prayer and devotion, of silence and spiritual friendship.

Pusey speaks in this letter of love as 'a wonderful thing', nothing less than 'a spark out of the boundless, shoreless ocean of His Fire of Love', and he goes on:

> You, I hope, are ripening continually. God ripen you more and more. Each day is a day of growth. God says to you 'Open thy mouth and I will fill it.' Only long. He does not want our words. The parched soil by its cracks, opens itself for the rain from heaven and invites it. The parched soul cries out to the living God. Oh then long and long and long, and God will fill thee. More love, more love, more love.[18]

The last words of the letter – its writer was eighty-two – speak eloquently of the sense of *epektasis*, that eager looking forward, that constant growth of the human person into the fulness of God, that continual journey further on into the boundless, shoreless ocean of God's love. They open up the way ahead. The teaching about deification shows itself to be anything but theoretical. It is lived and experienced through the self-surrender and the aspiration of a lifetime.

There is also in this sermon a new sense of the cosmic and mediatorial vocation of humankind as a whole, which comes out particularly in relation to the resurrection of the body, and the part which the body has in our apprehension of the divine glory. It is in the body that we stand in solidarity with the whole material creation. All this God has taken into himself, in sharing man's bodily condition of weakness and limitation: 'O marvellous device of divine wisdom and love, uniting things lowest with the highest, human with the divine, through our nature, the least and last and sunken lower still, raising up the whole universe into union with himself, encircling and enfolding all with his love, and knitting all in one; and that, through us!'[19]

As he meditates on the bliss of heaven in these sermons, Pusey constantly returns to the thought that there will be an infinite progress in love and knowledge, into the very life and being of God. Not surprisingly the idea of the divine beauty comes back forcefully, and it is interesting to see how Pantycelyn's insight, that the love which unites us with God must be as eternal as God himself, must *be* in fact God himself, is repeated here. The formulas which Pusey uses are surely the result of his own immediate experience, not only of his wide patristic reading.

> And so may the soul the more for ever delight itself in the sight of God, because it shall see him truly, yet cannot grasp him wholly. Where shall be an end of loving, where love is endless, infinite? or of gazing on Beauty infinite, when that very beauty

by our longing and its sight shall draw us more into itself; where is no weariness, no satiety, but a blessed union of thirst and satisfying fulness; where desire shall have no pang or void, and fulness shall but uphold desire; for both shall be perfect, unfailing love, unfailing through God's gift, as the very essence of God, who is love. If God who is the source of love can fail, then might the bliss of those fail, who see him, love him in himself.[20]

In his light alone shall we see light.

Again the thought of man's participation in God as a consequence of God's indwelling in man carries with it the thought that all creation participates in God in the measure which is appropriate to it. Here Pusey takes up the idea of God as light and life to all things, not only in the words of St Paul but also in those of one of the greatest of the early theologians of the Church, St Irenaeus.

'Thy eyes shall see the King in his beauty', yet not then, as far off, but brought nigh, yea within God. Even now, 'in him we live and move and have our being;' both by nature since he is everywhere, and there is no place out of God; and more blessedly by his providence which compasses us around, and by his grace dwells within our souls; 'and we live in him as in life Eternal.' But how much more there, where is the fulness of his presence, and we shall see him, who now also is around us, although we see him not. 'For', says an early Father, 'as they who behold the light are within the light and partake of its brightness, so they who behold God are within God, partaking of his brightness. For the brightness gives them life; they shall partake of life, beholding God. The beginning of life comes from the partaking of God; and to partake of God is to know God, and enjoy his goodness. Men then shall see God that they may live, by that sight made immortal and reaching unto God.'[21]

III

It is not to be thought that these sermons were preached by a man living a life of peaceful and untroubled contemplation. They were preached by a man hard-pressed within and without, passing through painful experiences of guilt and loss, and through frightening periods of self-hatred and self-reproach. Outwardly he found himself involved in unlooked for controversy and dispute, already knowing what it was to be isolated and deeply unpopular. It is out of his weakness, out of his self-despair that Pusey preaches in these ecstatic tones. We become aware of something of the sense of conflict within him in the last sermon in the series, on the need for a daily growth in grace:

> 'Fearfully indeed and wonderfully are we made'; a marvel to the blessed angels and to ourselves. Strange, out of what death those of us who shall live are brought into what life! What conflicting passions, feelings, appetites, powers, cravings, shall all have been fashioned by God's moulding hand, until they all be gathered and curiously wrought together into one, as being held together by him who is one, all centre in one, and so, in his unity to whom they tend, become one. Strange, through what variety of accidents, griefs, joys, terrors, fears, death, life his encircling providence girding us round, shall have fenced in our way; and he who has all creation at his command, shall have made all creation, good and bad, great and small, natural and moral, the holiness of angels and men and the malice of Satan, work together to the salvation of his elect.[22]

If a passionate concern for unity, for the one, is characteristic of mystics in all religious traditions, then indeed we should be right to recognise the mystical quality of these sermons. 'Never', wrote Owen Chadwick, 'would you naturally use the word *ecstatic* of the published writings of Keble or Newman, not even when reading their poetry. The word springs naturally to the mind of one reading the sermons of Pusey.'[23] We recall von Balthasar's definition of 'the double and reciprocal *ekstasis* – God's venturing forth to man and man's to God' as constituting the very content of dogmatics. In Pusey's preaching we have the raw material for such a truly catholic and unitive theology.

The Co-inherence of Human and Divine

The Christian tradition is thus full of an affirmation of God's nearness to humankind, and of our unrealised potential for God. The basic affirmations that Jesus is Lord, Jesus is the Christ, are affirmations about the possibilities of man, about the intimacy of relationship between human and divine, no less than about the mystery of God. They speak about a meeting, a union of God with humankind which alters our understanding, our deepest experience of what it is to be human, which gives us a new vision of the whole creation and alters the substance of our living and dying. They open up the full meaning of our calling to become partakers of the divine nature, to become sons in the one Son, to be filled with the Holy Spirit. They speak of deification. In this book we have been looking at this theme in a number of representative writers of the Anglican tradition since the Reformation. In this concluding chapter we shall look further at its expression as we find it in scripture and in earlier periods of the Christian tradition, and we shall reflect on it in relation to the mystery of God's joy in his creation, a joy which draws out from man a response of joy, a cry of praise and adoration. As Schmemann wrote, 'What the Church brought into the world was not certain ideas applicable to human needs, but first of all the truth, the righteousness, the joy of the Kingdom of God.' This joy is a liberating force which breaks the categories which can bind down and destroy our human life, both personal and social. It is a joy which unites heart and mind, will and understanding in a single ec-static movement of knowledge and of love.

I

Hidden in the margin of a ninth-century manuscript in the University Library in Cambridge there are some verses written in old Welsh. They are indeed one of the earliest surviving texts to be preserved in this the older of the two languages which inhabit the island of Britain. They speak to us of praise:

The world cannot express all thy glories,
   O true Lord,
Even if the grass and the trees were to sing . . .
Letters cannot contain them, letters cannot
   express them . . .
He who made the wonder of the world, will save us,
   has saved us.
It is not too great toil to praise the Trinity
It is not too great toil to praise the Son of Mary.[1]

The glory of God always goes beyond the words of men. No words, no letters, no books can express it. His glory overflows on every side. The whole universe is filled with the operations of his glory, but the whole universe cannot contain them. God who is wholly present in his world is yet totally transcendent of it. His immanence and his transcendence far from being opposed to one another, support and illuminate one another. It is in his immanence, his presence at the heart of this world, that we begin to glimpse the nature of his transcendence, he who comes out of himself into the pain, the sorrow, the darkness of his creation and fills it and redeems it.

The writer of the Fourth Gospel concludes his work with words which we too little consider, words which take up again the universal vision of the prologue of his book: 'There is much else that Jesus did. If it were all to be recorded in detail, I suppose the whole world would not hold the books that would be written' (John 21:25).

God's glory is at work in all things. Everything that exists, exists because it is held, sustained, enlivened by God's wisdom and God's power. The Word of God who is God, God expressing himself towards his creation, wills at all times to work the mystery of his embodiment. All things were made by God's eternal Word, all things hold together in him. In all things he wills to make himself known. And what is true of all things is still more true of humankind placed at the heart of this creation to give voice to its universal song of praise and to receive the presence of this glory with thanksgiving. So in the world of that unknown ninth-century Welsh writer, a world in its own way as threatened and precarious as our own – the pressures of the English to the East, the marauding raids of Vikings to the West – 'it is not too great toil to praise the Trinity; it is not too great toil to praise the Son of Mary'.

For the glory of God descends into the world, broods over the world, cherishes the world. It is so in the biblical account of creation, 'God saw all that he had made, and it was very good' (Gen. 1:31). The Lord rejoices over his works, and man can share in his rejoicing. From one of the latest writings of the Old Testament we hear the same thing:

> How beautiful is all that he has made, down to the smallest spark that can be seen! His works endure, all of them active for ever and all responsive to their various purposes. All things go in pairs, one opposite of the other; he has made nothing incomplete. One thing supplements the virtues of another; who could ever contemplate his glory enough? (Ecclus. 42:22–25)

We note with interest the suggestion of Yin and Yang in the pages of Holy Scripture: 'However much we say, we cannot exhaust our theme; to put it in a word, he is all. Where can we find the skill to sing his praises? For he is greater than all his works' (Ecclus. 43:27–28). He is in all; he *is* all, the writer is not afraid to say it, but at once he goes on to say that he is greater than all. His glory overflows, transcends our powers of praise and response.

But God's delight in his creation is focused in his dearly loved humankind. He longs for his people, delights to dwell among them, finds in them his joy. In the seventh century BC the prophet Zephaniah, having announced the day of God's judgement at length and with great emphasis, ends with a promise of deliverance. 'The Lord your God is in your midst, like a warrior to keep you safe; he will rejoice over you and be glad, he will rest over you in love, he will exult over you with a shout of joy' (Zeph. 3:17). God whose judgement is terrible, who brings down all that is proud, is above all a God of mercy. Three times the prophet repeats the affirmation of God's joy over his people. First it is said that he rejoices over us and is glad, then that he is silent and still in his joy, finally that he exults over us with exultation. The word in the original has associations with singing and dancing. For God too words are inadequate. We need to think of the silence of a love which is too deep for words, and the exultation of a joy which can be expressed in music and dance, rather than in speech.

Commenting on this passage in one of his sermons, E. B. Pusey is struck by the way in which God condescends to speak of his love for us in terms of our human love for one another, 'shadows out of his love to us sinners' in terms of the deepest love which he has given us:

> All holy love shadows forth some portion of his; Father, Mother, Husband would he be to the soul in his protecting, fostering, in-oneing love; and as our intensest love and joy cannot be uttered in words, but joy vents itself in unformed sounds, and love rests in silence over the object of its love, so he saith, 'he

will rejoice over us with the cry of jubilee, he will be still over us in love.'[2]

And this silence of God over his people, Pusey sees as an image of the everlasting silence of joy with which from all eternity the Father rests in his Son, the Word who is with him from all eternity. This language about the joy of the Father which rests in the Son needs to be taken fully seriously. We need to recognise in this joy which is at the heart of the Deity and overflows into creation, the presence and power of the Holy Spirit himself. Indeed, as St Gregory Palamas declares, 'The eternal joy of the Father and the Son is the Holy Spirit', the Holy Spirit whose presence is known in a silence which transcends all words, which goes beyond the capacity of words to limit and define, yet is at the same time the Spirit who spoke and who speaks by the prophets.

God can only speak to us, and we can only speak to God, and of God, in words which our human life has given us. Because those words are always too small, too limited, too fragile to express the fulness of his being and his joy, we have to seek ways by which we may expand them, allow them to carry more weight, to hold together a greater wealth of meaning and experience than they would normally do. This is one reason why much of the language of faith and prayer is the language of poetry, language which is, as we say, inspired. It is the quality of poetry to bring together, to concentrate in one word, one image, a great variety of meanings, many depths of signification. This is even more true of the sung word than of the spoken word, and this is why chant has been traditionally the vehicle of the Church's confession of faith, no less than of its praise. Song deepens and unites both our feeling and our understanding, bringing us together into a joy which is truth-telling and affirmative of life. The tradition of church music has a deeper theological significance than we normally acknowledge. 'The melody makes the words shared and loved, the words themselves being the dynamic basis of the infinite wealth of meaning which is expressed through the melody.'[3] The praise which is sung to God in psalms and hymns and spiritual songs is not something empty, less significant than the clearly delimited formulas of prose; it is not a mere inarticulate cry. It includes a fulness of meaning which overflows the definitions of the words, and makes them express more than we would have believed possible. This is what it is to sing with the Spirit and to sing with understanding, to praise in the power of him who is himself the joy of the Father and the Son.

At times this fulness of joy goes beyond all formulations into the silence of contemplation, and into the exultation of praise. Of

silence it is best to say little, beyond underlining its necessity. All
our words spoken about God, spoken to God, should be qualified
by silence, should proceed from silence and proceed to silence, the
silence of contemplative prayer and adoration. But on the question
of the exultation which goes beyond words in their usual conno-
tations there is perhaps more to say. In the sermon already quoted
Pusey refers to a remarkable passage in Augustine where he speaks
of the way in which human joy in God can sometimes go beyond
words:

> Think of people as they go about some hot and exhausting job
> – at harvest time say, or in the vineyard. They start celebrating
> their happiness with the words of familiar songs. But they end
> up turning away from words and syllables, as if they were filled
> with so much happiness that they couldn't put it into words.
> And off they go into the noise of jubilation. This kind of singing
> is a sound which means that the heart is giving birth to something
> it cannot speak of. And who better to receive such jubilation
> than the ineffable God – ineffable, because you cannot talk about
> him? And if you cannot talk about him, and it is improper just
> to keep silence, why, what is there left for you to do but jubilate
> – with your heart rejoicing without words, and the immense
> breadth of your joy not rationed out in syllables.[4]

Such a passage forcibly suggests the need for a deeper and more
consistent theological reflection than is usual on the phenomena
associated with the contemporary movements of renewal going on
in the Church of the West. The experience of praise and joy in the
life and prayer of the Christian people can tell us much about the
way in which God goes beyond our words and categories. The
practice of singing in tongues, for instance, might bring us to a
new understanding of the ineffability of God, and of the properly
apophatic nature of all theological language.

God can only be spoken of by us, God can only speak to us, in
terms of human experience; but it is that experience at its most
intense, most complete, most compelling; men and women
involved in hard but rewarding common labour, rejoicing in
bringing it to completion, or the protecting, fostering, in-oneing
love of father, mother, husband, wife. It is at a wedding feast that
he can turn the water of our life in time into the wine of his
kingdom of eternity. It is thus that God speaks to us of his love
for us. It is thus that he will rejoice over this whole creation, and
over every part of it, joying over the creation and deliverance of
each one of his children, for there is joy in the presence of the
angels over one sinner that repents.

II

This theme of joy has a central place in the New Testament, no less in the gospels than in the epistles, but it is one which is not generally considered sufficiently in depth. For our purposes it has particular importance because, as well as speaking of the way in which the Word of God goes beyond all human words, it stresses something of the reciprocity of the divine and human exchange. God joys in his creation; he rejoices over finding what had been lost. But man joys in God, in communion with his fellow human beings, and in union with all creation. One of the most powerful of all the images in the gospels is that of a great feast, the feast of the kingdom of eternity. In its joys all the participants share. Of course the reciprocity is, in one sense, not complete. God is creator, man creature; God is infinite, man finite; God is eternal, man temporal. But in another sense the reciprocity is full and all-embracing, for between the two there is love, knowledge, communion, joy, and these are things which are shared to the uttermost. God goes out of himself to man and man to God in return. All creation is intended to be the place where God's glory dwells, and within that creation God has chosen his dearly loved humankind to be the heart of his indwelling.

Considerations such as these can help us to understand better the context in which the affirmations of faith in Jesus as the Son of God, which we find in the New Testament, should be placed. They are to be understood within an intense and lived experience, both personal and corporate, of the union and communion, the fusion in love, of man with God, and of men and women with one another in God. They proceed from a living knowledge of co-inherence and exchange, in which it does not seem strange to speak of us as living in one another, or of God as living in us and we in him. Christ is in us, we are in him. In him there is a new creation. It is true that in the New Testament Jesus is always portrayed as in some vital way unique, and this uniqueness has been respected throughout the Christian tradition. But this uniqueness is of an inclusive and not an exclusive kind; for what he is all his fellow men and women are called to become. It is true that the creeds speak of his coming down to earth from heaven, but he does not come down as an alien intruder, but as the one in whom the whole movement of God's descent into his world is focused. Furthermore he comes down in order that he may raise us up. The language of incarnation, of God's taking flesh, is in the faith and understanding of the early Christian centuries, and indeed until today wherever that faith and understanding are alive, balanced and completed by the language of man's inspiration, his being indwelt by the Holy

Spirit, and by the language of his deification, his becoming God by God's gift and grace. Indeed without the reciprocity implied in the language of deification and in the language about the Holy Spirit as the power, the wisdom and the joy of God, overflowing into his creation, we can hardly make sense of the language of incarnation at all. Unless we affirm with Athanasius that God became man in order that man might become God, the language of incarnation is likely to lose its true significance, as unfortunately it too often has done.

In saying this it is not suggested that there is no need for new formulations, for creative reinterpretations of the tradition which we have received. Indeed to speak of 'receiving the tradition' can itself be a misleading way of putting things, if it suggests that there is anything passive or inert about the process. To live, to think through, to experience the tradition anew involves at all times an effort of new creation. As Vladimir Lossky would say, 'Christian truth is not neutral ground, it is a conquest.' In the light of our changing understanding of our human nature, and of the world around us, in the light of our much closer involvement with the other religious traditions of humankind, this need is particularly evident. But this effort is likely to be frustrated if it begins with a failure to see what the tradition in its fulness has been saying; if we begin, that is, by rejecting as 'classical Christology' what is no more than a caricature of the teaching of the Christian thinkers who lived in the centuries when those classical formulations were taking form. Unfortunately a good deal of re-thinking of the tradition has started from this point, that is, from the supposition that the development of the doctrines of the Trinity and the incarnation in the early Christian centuries marked the intrusion of abstract and alien Greek ways of thought into the power and simplicity of the original gospel message. It has been the purpose of this book to suggest that the contrary is the case, that when these doctrines are seen in their true significance, in relation to the doctrine of man's deification in Christ through the Spirit, then they may be seen to express and safeguard the very heart of the New Testament message of the reconciliation and union of God and man. The experienced and saving faith proclaimed by the Wesleys, for instance, demands the doctrine of the Trinity and the incarnation as its framework and articulation, as the Wesleys themselves clearly saw.

To illustrate these contentions we shall turn to the teaching of one of the greatest though still one of the least known of the theologians of the eastern tradition, Maximus the Confessor, to see a little of what the doctrine of the incarnation will say to us in his hands. And first of all it must be said that Maximus is one of those thinkers who want to draw everything together into unity. In our Anglican tradition Richard Hooker is perhaps the closest parallel. Maximus had read widely in all his predecessors, and by the seventh century of the Christian era when he lived he was in a position to draw together into a synthesis strands from the very varying schools of thought which had flourished in the centuries before him. He is by the common consent of those who have studied him most deeply a theologian whose thought is shaped and controlled by the Chalcedonian definition of the union of God with man in Christ, a union without confusion, a maintenance of distinction without separation, a union of co-inherence and exchange. Maximus has a remarkably consistent, but a remarkably subtle mind. Here is the central point of his reflection.

We have thought that the element of reciprocity in the Christian story of our humanity's being taken into God, no less than of God's entering our humanity, is a point which has often been neglected in more recent centuries in the theology of the West. For a variety of reasons, both in Catholicism and in Protestantism, the language of deification has been held in some suspicion. Our Anglican theologians are something of an exception in their readiness to use it. In Maximus however the quality of reciprocity is marked indeed. There is an exchange between God and man; on that he insists. And in him there is an equally strong insistence on the all-inclusive nature of the divine initiative in Christ. All human history has been moving to this point, all human history is touched and changed by it. I quote from a passage in which he is speaking of the power of love, the love of God in the love of man and the love of man in the love of God, to draw things together into one. He speaks of:

> the power of this reciprocal gift which deifies man for God through the love of God, and makes God man for man through his love for man, making through this noble exchange God to become man for the deification of man, and man to become God for the humanisation of God. For the Word of God who is God wills always and in all things to work the mystery of his embodiment.[5]

The Word of God is at work in all things. It is the clear affirmation of the New Testament writers. Maximus takes it and articulates it in his own particular fashion. He sees the whole creation as full of the *words* of God, God's creative and dynamic intentions and will for his creation. These *words* in their almost infinite diversity are gathered together and find their fulfilment in the one Word who is God, thus allowing God to manifest his glory and his love throughout creation. But in this process we ourselves have a crucial part to play. We are placed in the midst of this material world, ourselves part of it, yet with the capacity to go beyond it. We are part of the world; Maximus insists much on the importance of the body which links us with that world and with all our fellow human beings, and on the part which it plays in our journey towards God. Humankind is placed in this focal position in creation with the task of bringing this work to completion, of being the place in which this noble exchange of human and divine can take place. 'In his way to union with God, man in no way leaves creatures aside, but gathers together in his love the whole cosmos disordered by sin, that it may at last be transfigured by grace.'[6]

What more precisely does Maximus have in mind when he speaks of God being humanised, made man? He speaks of *the* incarnation of course; 'the Word was made flesh and dwelt among us'. But that is not an isolated incident. It is a focal point for all creation. So when he speaks of incarnation Maximus speaks of much more. We share in the nature of God, become partakers of the divine nature, and God shares in our nature, expresses himself in our humanity, as little by little we learn to live a life of active and suffering love, thus sharing in God's own love. By the action of God's grace, which is no created affect of God's action but is God himself at work in us, we become sharers in his nature and he in ours. The most authoritative interpreter of Maximus in our time, the Romanian theologian Fr Dumitru Staniloae, puts it like this:

The most shining demonstration of the action of grace within us is in our sympathetic awareness of our neighbour. By grace we long to make those who are in need at home with us, as we wish to make God at home with us. Nothing contributes so much to our growth in righteousness, to our drawing close to God, to our deification, as compassion showed to those in need. If the Word has said that those who suffer are God [the reference is to the parable in Matt. 25, where the Son of Man says that it was he who was hungry and naked and in prison, in those who have suffered in these ways], much more shall they be accounted God by grace who practice giving and thus make God's gracious activity their own.

God suffers in those who suffer, taking their pain into himself, but God heals in those who heal, in those who show by their actions that they share God's own perception and understanding of things. 'Maximus uses the doctrine of the uncreated energies of God to underline the fact that God holds us all together with himself, by reason of his active suffering with all . . . For the energies of God are not shut in on themselves, but come out into the world, and are active throughout creation.[7] By our action in service of others we make these energies our own, and thus the whole of the human family is bound together by the action of God energising in the action of man, the suffering of God at work in the suffering of man, the love of God in the love of man.

In this way the deifying grace of God enters into the simplest of human actions, a cup of cold water given to a child, a visit made to someone in sickness. Of course the Godward dimensions of such actions need not be conscious. In the gospel passage cited they are evidently not, but the divine transcendence and the divine immanence are brought very close together in them, and things which are called mysticism and spirituality are directly related to things which we call social and political concern. The incarnation of the Word of God at Bethlehem, in Galilee, in Jerusalem, is not an insolated wonder, but a central focal point in a network of divine initiatives which spreads out into the whole of human history, indeed into the whole universe. The story of Jesus is the story of the meeting of God with man and of man with God. It is a story which is yet completed. It begins with the initiative of God, which has its origins solely in him. But for its proper telling it will always need to be told in two ways, both from the Godward and from the manward side. It needs from the human point of view to be seen in relation to the whole previous history of man, not only to the history of the people of Israel, which lies directly behind it, and also in relation to the whole subsequent history of humankind, of which your history and mine is a part. It is a story which will lead us to reflect on the ec-static nature of God and man, on the mystery that God is a God who can come out of himself and dwell in man; that we human beings are creatures who can come out of ourselves and dwell in God, indeed creatures who can only truly become ourselves by going beyond ourselves, can only become fully human by finding ourselves in God. There is within our nature an infinite and unbounded capacity for God. God can joy in man and man in God.

And man participates in God, and God participates in man, not only through deeds of active compassion, through the deepening of our human solidarity with one another. There is also a more hidden, intimate relationship between God and man, which forms the heart of that activity we call prayer, and without which no true growth in interhuman solidarity is ultimately possible. Here again there is a reciprocity and co-inherence deeper than we think. Prayer is not our shouting to a distant indifferent God. As a contemporary poet, R. S. Thomas, puts it:

> It begins to appear
> this is not what prayer is about.
> It is the annihilation of difference,
> the consciousness of myself in you
> of you in me . . .[8]

We have to realise, in the words of an outstanding American spiritual father:

> that we *are* the glory of God . . . We live because we share God's breath, God's life, God's glory. Take this as your *koan*; 'I am the glory of God' . . . You are the place where God chooses to dwell, you are the *topos tou theou* (God's place) and the spiritual life is nothing more or less than to allow that space to exist where God can dwell, to create the space where his glory can manifest itself.[9]

Such affirmations have almost unlimited implications for our understanding of the nature of man and of the nature of the God who is pleased to dwell in him. There must be in man, if he is to become the dwelling place of God, the capacity:

> of assimilating a consciousness of infinite depth and radiance . . . Man must be capable of continually renewing and deepening his conscious experience of God, and God in his turn must delight in this perpetual renewal of his joy in the man in whom he rests. Man must be always responding anew to the experience of God, for only if he does can God himself have the joy of continually resting in man . . . That is what is meant by the divinisation of man in God, and the humanisation of God in man. It is the union of God and man in the Holy Spirit, the Spirit of light . . . By affirming that this mutual penetration without confusion occurs between God and man, Christianity has revealed the unfathomable and indefinable mystery of the human person and his consciousness.[10]

It is worth remarking that this way of seeing the depth of our personal existence comes from a theologian who for forty years has lived in the Communist half of our world, a man acutely conscious of the human realities of the twentieth century, painful as well as joyful. We have here a genuine response to the anguish as well as to the achievement of our time.

III

It is in the light of such an understanding of both God and man that we can begin to understand the meaning of all incarnation, as well as *the* incarnation, can begin to see the links between the activity of the uncreated light which is in every man, and the light which shines supremely in the face of Jesus Christ. At the moment of his baptism, the inauguration of his public ministry, Jesus goes down into the water, the element from which life came, accepts identification with the history of our race, stands in solidarity with all his fellow human beings as well as with the faith and expectation of the people to whom he belongs. As he comes up out of the water he sees 'the heavens torn open and the Spirit like a dove descending upon him. And a voice spoke from heaven, Thou art my Son, my Beloved; on thee my favour rests' (Mark 1:10–11). There is a uniqueness here. There is one Father, one Spirit, one Son, one Beloved. But this is an all-inclusive oneness, for it is the oneness of the source of all creation, all healing, all transformation, all fulfilment. God joys in his creation, in the work of his hands. The Father holds out his hands of love, the Son and the Spirit, to welcome all creation. The circulation of love which is in God through all eternity opens itself to embrace all things, to touch and heal the pain, the sorrow, the lostness of man. We think of the most famous of the icons of the Orthodox East, the Holy Trinity of Andrei Rublev, to which we have already referred. It is an icon which is everywhere disclosing its presence in the West. The three angels are seated round a table, but the circle is open to include us, and at the centre of the table, and at the centre of the picture, is the symbol of sacrificial love.

We observe that in St Mark's account of the baptism of Jesus it is said that the heavens are *torn* open. At the heart of the Trinity in the Rublev icon is the dish with the slain lamb, the symbol of sacrifice. The glory of God is most fully revealed in the man on the cross of Golgotha. Here we see the lengths to which the love of God in the love of man, the love of man in the love of God can go. This is what we mean when we speak of the ec-static nature of that love, a love which carries us beyond ourselves.

God acts, offers, gives, in order to bring creation into fellowship with him; and because that fellowship is so strange to fearful, self-enclosed human beings, it requires a uniquely creative gift, a gift which involves God manifesting himself without power or threats. He 'distances' himself from the stability of his divine life in order to share the vulnerability and darkness of mortal men and women. By the 'gift' of his presence in our world of unreserved compassion and unrestricted hope – he establishes communion; but this can be clearly shown only in conditions of final rejection and dereliction. The gift is consummated on the cross.[11]

It is hard for the good pleasure of God to break through the walls of man's complacency and self-sufficing. The joy of the Spirit is a violent joy, which brings sorrow with it, a painful, searing grief which reveals the waste, the tragedy, the frustration, the destructiveness of human life, when lived apart from the source of all life. The darkness is seen most sharply when the potential of God's glory and delight is revealed. This darkness has never been more apparent in human history than today. It is true that the human condition has always been threatened by forces which enslave, by a power which kills and destroys. The temptation for man to choose death rather than life, curse rather than blessing is as old as the human race. But since August 1945 we have had in our hands an actual power to destroy that we have never had before. The issues of life and death are sharpened to an intolerable degree. We find it almost impossible to think of the capacities for destruction which we have developed, 'the virtually incalculable destructive power of nuclear weapons'.[12]

At a moment of such intense conflict in human history, how is the light of God to be perceived? How is the joy of God, the delight of God in man and in creation to be made known? How can that joy become at this moment in history, the century of Auschwitz and Hiroshima, the reality which dwells not only in the heart of each one of us but also at the heart of the whole of humankind, how can it inhabit the central place of the whole human family? Very evidently it cannot happen through any abdication of our responsibility for the things of this world, a pietistic withdrawal into some imagined sphere of religious invulnerability. Rather we need to face together the issues which God himself sets before us in our time. There is the question of the control of the destructive powers which technology has given us, powers to destroy, suddenly or more gradually, the very possibilities of future life on this planet. We cannot hide from ourselves the fact that the forces which make against true humanity are frightening in their power. In the Communist world it is evident that the developed system of dialectical materialism is at enmity with human freedom as it is with joy. It can imprison man in a sombre and corrupt bureaucracy. But it is evident that the practical materialism of the capitalist West is no less destructive in its quieter, more insidious way. In western Europe and North America alike it manifests itself in an always strengthening idolatry of money, in an ideology which makes considerations of financial profit and loss determinative at every level of society, and which therefore can have little regard for things which are not subject to such forms of measurement, let alone for the condition of the poor, the old, the weak, the wounded. In both societies we see a frightening contempt for what is human, a contempt which is rooted in our contempt for God. Only in the rediscovery of the co-inherence of God with man and man with God can we respond to the extremity of this situation. Linked with this is the need for a new discovery of the mystery of human co-inherence which lies at the heart of the gospel; that we are all one in Christ Jesus; that each one of us is everyman; that the whole history of the human race is, in a hidden way, recapitulated in the life of each one of us. The inclusive uniqueness of the person of the Christ reveals to us the unfathomable mystery and uniqueness of each human person.

This is why while there can be no place among Christians for an abandonment of our share in responsibility for the public issues of our day, there is also an urgent need for a rediscovery of the inner depth in each one, that inner depth in which we find the presence of God within us, and finding that, find all our fellow women and men in it. Again what we call mysticism cannot be separated from what we call politics. The churches of the West, which have terribly neglected this inner experiential element of our heritage, have a particular and urgent responsibility to rediscover its fulness. It is this which will enable us to make a true response to the religions of the East, to Buddhism and Hinduism. This is a rediscovery which will also involve a new appreciation of the fragility and beauty of the things of this earth, a new realisation of our unity with all our fellow human beings, and a new sense of God's utter transcendence made known in his complete immanence. There is a promise of a new heart, a new mind, a new birth in the Spirit now in this moment of crisis and judgement, which like all such movements in our human history, whether personal or universal, is also a moment when God's creative energy longs to be revealed, when the divine energies are already powerfully at work bringing to birth the reality of a new creation.

For the things which belong to the story of Jesus are not yet completed. The once for all event of the coming of the Christ is an event which opened the way towards a future, whose fulness is not yet made known. One of the early Cistercian fathers, Isaac of Stella, by birth an Englishman, by adoption French, speaks of the three births of Christ, the first from all eternity from God, the second in time from his mother and the third which he shares with us and we with him in the power of the Spirit:

This third birth is also in the context of time, but it will last for all eternity . . . Yes, the birth of Christ, his life, death, resurrection and ascension have indeed begun, but they are not yet brought to completion; beginning with the first man and ending with the last, they are spread over all the history that intervenes . . .[13]

The death and resurrection of Christ have indeed begun but they are not yet completed. Christ is to be born, to die, to rise and to ascend in the history of all humankind, and in the history of each one of us. Small wonder that if all the things which Jesus did were to be written down the world itself could not contain the books that would be written.

At the heart of our world, at the heart of each one of us, God wills to dwell. He rejoices over this world with a joy which is unspeakable, a joy which liberates and sustains, which cleanses and redeems the lost potential of each human heart and of all creation. Now in this late-twentieth century the Church turns to him in prayer for the coming of the Spirit, who is Lord and lifegiver, who will renew the face of this ravaged earth, the ravaged earth which lies around our great, but so ambiguous cities, the ravaged earth which is the very life of each one of us. In the descent of God's joy into the centre of our world, man's spirit leaps up into union with God's Spirit, the world's own power of life is released, its responsive and creative power rises up and participates in that eternal movement of love which is at the very heart of God himself.

Notes

Introduction

1. The statement in this form is found in Athanasius, *De Incarnatione*, 54. For a clear account of the doctrine in its Eastern Orthodox form see G. I. Mantzaridis, *The Deification of Man: St Gregory Palamas and Orthodox Tradition*. New York, 1984.
2. *Anglican-Orthodox Dialogue* (London, 1984), p. 50.
3. I am not of course claiming Pantycelyn as a representative of the English tradition, though it is worth mentioning that he is described on the title page of the collected edition of his hymns (1811) as a 'Minister of the Church of England'. But the existence of Wales is an important part of the forgotten history of this island of Britain and for any adequate and genuinely new realisation of what it is to be English, some knowledge of the Welsh tradition would seem to be very nearly indispensable.
4. See below p. 59.
5. *Sobornost*, vol. 7, no. 1 (1985), p. 13.
6. See the article by R. D. Williams, 'Deification' in *A Dictionary of Christian Spirituality*, ed. G. S. Wakefield. London, 1983.
7. John Meyendorff, *Byzantine Theology* (New York, 1974), pp. 225-6.

Chapter 2   The Mystery of Endless Union: Richard Hooker and Lancelot Andrewes

1. T. S. Eliot, *For Lancelot Andrewes: essays on style and order* (1928), p. 17.
2. C. S. Lewis, *English Literature in the Sixteenth Century, excluding drama* (Oxford, 1954), p. 460.
3. Maximus the Confessor. See below p. 70.
4. Richard Hooker, *Laws of Eccles. Pol.*, I, xi, 2, in *Works*, ed. John Keble (1836), vol. I.
5. ibid. I, xi, 3.
6. ibid. I, xi, 4.
7. ibid. I, xi, 6.
8. ibid.
9. C. S. Lewis, *Transpositions and Other Essays* (1946), p. 31.

10. Olivier Loyer, *L'Anglicanisme de Richard Hooker* (Paris, 1979), vol. I, pp. 353 ff.
11. ibid. pp. 378–9.
12. Hooker, *Laws of Eccles. Pol.*, V, l, 3, in *Works*, vol. II.
13. ibid. V, lvi, 7.
14. From a sermon of Ralph Cudworth preached in March 1647, qu. in *Anglicanism*, ed. P. E. More and F. L. Cross (London, 1951), pp. 782–3. I have transliterated the Greek.
15. R. W. Church, *Pascal and Other Sermons* (1896), p. 62.
16. *For Lancelot Andrewes*, pp. 29–30.
17. Lancelot Andrewes, *Complete Works. Library of Anglo-Catholic Theology* (1841–54), vol. I, p. 122.
18. ibid.
19. Nicholas Lossky, *Lancelot Andrewes: Le Predicateur* (Paris, 1986), pp. 157–8.
20. ibid. pp. 326–7.
21. ibid. p. 327.
22. Lancelot Andrewes, op.cit. vol. III, pp. 108–9.
23. ibid. p. 367.
24. Lossky, op.cit. p. 327.

Chapter 3   Man as God and God as Man: Charles Wesley and Williams Pantycelyn

1. *A Rapture of Praise: Hymns of John and Charles Wesley*, ed. H. A. Hodges and A. M. Allchin (London 1968), 5, pp. 58–9; *Methodist Hymn Book* (1933), no. 142.
2. *A Rapture of Praise*, 27, pp. 74–5; MHB, 299.
3. RP, 131, p. 149.
4. John Wesley, *Large Hymn Book* (1780), introd.
5. Qu. in Virginia Woolf, *The Common Reader* (London, 1948), p. 13.
6. RP, 136, pp. 152–3.
7. Gregory Dix, *The Shape of the Liturgy* (London, 1945), pp. 29–30.
8. J. Ernest Rattenbury, *The Eucharistic Hymns of John and Charles Wesley* (London, 1948), pp. 154–6.
9. RP, 90, p. 123; MHB, 568. Even in a hymn intended for children Wesley will use such language: 'Loving Jesus, gentle Lamb,/ In thy gracious hand, I am;/ Make me Saviour what thou art,/ Live thyself within my heart.' EH, 591.
10. J. E. Rattenbury, *The Evangelical Doctrines of Charles Wesley's Hymns*, p. 63.
11. For instance, in the introduction to the *John Wesley* volume in the Library of Protestant Theology. New York, 1964.
12. *Eucharistic Hymns*, p. 212.
13. This point is further discussed in the Introduction to *A Rapture of Praise*, cf. pp. 33–6.
14. During the eighteenth century the Welsh dioceses formed part of the province of Canterbury as they had done for many centuries before.

Only in 1919 did the Church in Wales become an autonomous province of the Anglican communion.

15. G. M. Roberts, *Y Per Ganiedydd* (Pantycelyn) (Aberystwyth, 1949). vol. I, pp. 167–8.

16. ibid. pp. 105–6.

17. *Gwanwyn Duw, Diwygwyr a Diwygiadau*, ed. J. E. Wynn Davis (Caernarfon, 1982), pp. 143–63.

18. These translations and most of those used in this chapter I owe to the late Professor H. A. Hodges, a pioneer of Pantycelyn studies in England.

19. *Llyfr Emynau a Thonau* (Caernarfon/Bangor, 1929), 80.

20. ET.

21. *Gwanwyn Duw*, p. 152.

22. See the essay by Derec Llwyd Morgan in *Y Traddodiad Rhyddiaith*, ed. G. Bowen (Llandysul, 1970), pp. 293–317, in which he points to Pantycelyn's knowledge of this work of Edward Reynolds.

23. ET, 259.

24. *Y Per Ganiedydd*, p. 83.

25. This aspect of the movement has been particularly well described by Dr Derec Llwyd Morgan, both in his general study, *Y Diwygiad Mawr* (Llandysul, 1981), and in his more recent essay, 'Williams Pantycelyn' in the series *Lien y Llenor* (Caernarfon, 1983). I am indebted to both works and to the active encouragement of their author.

26. William Williams, *Gwaith Prydyeddawl* (Caerdyrddin, 1811), pp. 91–2. Translated, the title page of this edition by John Williams, Pantycelyn reads: 'The Poetic Work of the late Reverend William Williams of Pantycelyn, Minister of the Church of England; that is to say, all the hymns which the author composed together with certain texts.'

27. Quoted in the study by Glyn Tegai Hughes, *Williams Pantycelyn*, published in English in the series Writers of Wales (Cardiff, 1983), p. 18. The first serious introduction to Pantycelyn in English.

28. ibid. p. 89.

29. ET, 681.

30. Saunders Lewis, *Williams Pantycelyn* (1927), pp. 188–9.

31. These two verses are not in the current hymn book (ET). In the 1811 edition they are on p. 424.

32. See above p. 14.

33. A. M. Allchin, *Ann Griffiths*, ser. Writers of Wales (Cardiff, 1976), pp. 20–1.

34. Hans Urs von Balthasar, *The Glory of the Lord: a theological aesthetics* (Edinburgh, 1982), vol. I, pp. 125–6.

Chapter 4   A Life which is both His and Theirs: E. B. Pusey and the Oxford Movement

1. For Pusey's reaction to Newman's conversion see my essay, 'The idea of unity in Tractarian theology and spirituality' in Geoffrey Rowell (ed.), *Tradition Renewed* (1986).
2. Louis Bouyer, *Newman* (Paris, 1953), pp. 223f (my translation).
3. See Andrew Louth's essay, 'Manhood into God: the Oxford Movement, the fathers and the deification of man' in *Essays Catholic and Radical*, ed. Kenneth Leech and Rowan Williams (London, 1983), pp. 74–5.
4. Qu. in Geoffrey Rowell, *The Vision Glorious*. Oxford, 1983.
5. See my essay, 'The theological vision of the Oxford Movement' in *Newman: a portrait restored*, ed. J. Coulson and A. M. Allchin. London, 1966.
6. G. Rowell, *op. cit.*
7. These hymns in *English Hymnal*.
8. *A course of sermons on solemn subjects chiefly bearing on repentance and amendment of life, preached in S. Saviour's Church, Leeds, during the week after its consecration on the feast of S. Simon and S. Jude, 1845* (1845). Not all the sermons are by Pusey and so his name does not appear on the title page.
9. ibid. Sermon XVIII, pp. 309–29.
10. ibid. pp. 320–1.
11. ibid. pp. 323–9; for a further discussion of this passage see *Tradition Renewed*, ed. Rowell, op. cit.
12. J. K. Kadowaki, SJ, *Zen and the Bible: a priest's experience* (London, 1980), p. 98.
13. John the Solitary, 'On Prayer', ed. and tr. Sebastian Brock, *Journal of Theological Studies* (April 1979), vol. XXX, pt I.
14. See my essay, 'Pusey, the servant of God', in *Pusey Rediscovered*, ed. Percy Butler (London, 1983), p. 370.
15. *Sermons*, pp. 265–6.
16. ibid. pp. 266–7.
17. ibid.
18. The letter in in H. P. Liddon, *Life of E. B. Pusey*, vol. IV (1898), p. 376, though with no indication of who it was sent to. See also Peter Cobb, 'Dr Pusey and Sister Clara' in *The Fairacres Chronicle*, vol. 16, no. 1 (Spring 1983), pp. 4–15; and also T. J. Williams, *Lydia Priscilla Sellon*, 2nd edn, 1965.
19. *Sermons*, p. 294.
20. ibid. pp. 280–1.
21. ibid. p. 281.
22. ibid. p. 335.
23. Owen Chadwick, *The Mind of the Oxford Movement* (London, 1960), p. 49.

Chapter 5   The Co-inherence of Human and Divine

1. Ifor Williams, *The Beginnings of Welsh Poetry* (Cardiff, 1972), pp. 101–2, where the full text of these verses will be found together with Sir Ifor Williams' detailed comments on the language and the meaning of the text.

2. E. B. Pusey, *Sermons preached in St Saviour's Church, Leeds* (1845), p. 245.

3. Words of Dumitru Staniloae, qu. in A. M. Allchin, *The Living Presence of the Past* (New York, 1981), p. 85.

4. I have used the translation in R. D. Williams, *The Wound of Knowledge* (London, 1979), p. 87, rather than the more archaic translation which Pusey puts in his footnote.

5. A text from the *Ambigua* of Maximus. For an introduction to his work see Lars Thunberg, *Man and Cosmos; the theological vision of St Maximus the Confessor*. New York, 1985. On Maximus' anthropology Thunberg's earlier work, *Microcosm and Mediator* (Lund, 1965), is essential reading.

6. Words of Vladimir Lossky summing up the teaching of Maximus, in V. Lossky, *The Mystical Theology of the Eastern Church* (London, 1958), p. 111.

7. Maximus the Confessor, *Philosophical and Theological Questions*, vol. I, Introduction and commentary by D. Staniloae (Athens, 1978), pp. 248–9 (modern Greek).

8. R. S. Thomas, 'Emerging' in *Laboratories of the Spirit* (London, 1975), p. 1.

9. Fr John Eudes Bamberger, qu. in H. J. M. Nouwen, *The Genesee Diary* (New York, 1976), p. 53.

10. D. Staniloae, *Prayer and Holiness: the icon of man renewed in God* (Oxford, 1982), pp. 14–15.

11. R. D. Williams, *Eucharistic Sacrifice: the roots of a metaphor*, Grove Liturgical Study, no. 31 (Nottingham, 1982), p. 28.

12. From Church of England Report, *The Church and the Bomb*. London, 1982.

13. Louis Bouyer, *The Cistercian Heritage*, London 1966.

Index

Aleluia see Hymn books
Andrewes, Lancelot 3, 4, 7–23, 24, 47
Anglican–Orthodox Joint Doctrinal Commission 3
Anglican Spiritual Tradition (Moorman) 3
Anselm 54
Aquinas, St Thomas 25
Arnold, Thomas 16
Athanasian creed 36
Athanasius, St 5, 14, 69
Augustine, St 10, 46, 52
Auschwitz 75

Bamberger, John Eudes 73
Baptism 13, 17, 74
Beauty divine 10–12, 42–3, 60–1, 65
Bernard, St 42, 46, 54
Blake, William 3
'Bliss of Heaven' (Pusey) 57
Bonaventure 46
Bouyer, Louis 51
Brevint, Daniel, *Christian Sacrament and Sacrifice* 34
Brilioth, Yngve 54
British Critic see J. B. Mozley
Buddhism 1, 76
Byzantine rite 28

Calvinism 7
Catholic Doctrine of the Holy Trinity (Jones of Neyland) 34, 37
Chadwick, Owen 62
Chalcedon 13, 31, 70
Charles of Bala, Thomas 35–6
Christian Sacrament and Sacrifice (Brevint) 34
Christian Year see Hymn books
Chrysostom, St John 4
Clara, Sister (Clarissa Powell) 59
Co-inherence 6, 12–13, 17, 32, 58, 63–77

Cudworth, Ralph 14, 44
Cyprian, 52
Cyril of Alexandria 5, 52, 57–8

Damian, St Peter 59
Dix, Gregory 32

Ekstasis 5–6, 12, 16, 22, 27, 29–30, 45, 47, 54, 62, 72
Eliot, T. S. 7, 21–2; *For Lancelot Andrewes* 16; *Four Quartets* 22
Elizabeth I of England 7
English Spirituality (Thornton) 3
Ephrem, St 25
Eucharist 13, 15, 20, 29–30, 32–4, 45–6, 50, 55
Evangelicalism 26
Evangelical Movement 24, 48

Farewell Visible, Welcome Invisible Things see Hymn books
For Lancelot Andrewes (Eliot) 16
Four Quartets (Eliot) 22
Fox, George 3

Gregory Nazianzen 5
Gregory of Nyssa 46
Griffiths, Ann 45–6

Harris, Howell 35
Herbert, George 25
Herrlichkeit (von Balthasar) 46–7, 62
Hinduism 1, 76
Hiroshima 75
Hooker, Richard 2, 4, 7–23, 24, 43, 47, 70; *Laws of Ecclesiastical Polity* 7–23 *passim*
Hymn books
    Aleluia 40
    Christian Year 53
    Farewell Visible, Welcome Invisible Things 43

Hymns on the Lord's Supper 29
Large Hymn Book 30, 33
Hymns (first lines)
  Come, Holy Ghost, all-quickening
    fire 28
  He is my fair prince 40
  How glorious is the life above 29
  If here and now the beauty of your
    face 42
  In Eden, I shall always remember
    this 37
  It is a flame of fire from mid-most
    heaven 38
  Let earth and heaven combine 26
  O, a passionate, powerful, strong
    flame 38
  O blessed hour of eternal rest 46
  Plant in my soul every one 39
  See where our great High Priest 32
  Since the Son hath set me free 33
  The bonds of nature will all be
    broken 43
  Your beauty will be forever new 42

Irenaeus 19, 61
Isaac of Stella 76

James I of England 15
John, St (apostle) 51
John XXIII, pope 21
John of Damascus 25
Johannine teaching 6
John Paul II, pope 21
Johnson, Samuel 31
Johnston, William 57
Jones, R. Tudur 37–8
Jones of Neyland, William, *Catholic
  Doctrine of the Holy Trinity* 34,
  37
Jonson, Ben 7
Joy 4–5, 10, 18, 30, 43–5, 54, 58–9,
  63–7, 73–7
Julian of Norwich 3

Kadowaki, J. K. 56
Kant, Immanuel 39
Keble, John 4, 48–62 *passim*;
  Christian Year 53

Language, poetic 30–1, 37–8, 66
Large Hymn Book see Hymn books
Latin rite 28
Law, William 3
Law of Sinai 41

Laws of Ecclesiastical Polity
  (Hooker) 7–23 *passim*
Lectures on Justification
  (Newman) 51, 53
Lewis, C. S., 8, 9, 11; *Oxford History
  of English Literature* 8; 'The
  Weight of Glory' 12
Lewis, Saunders 43
Life, monastic 50, 56, 59
Lossky, Nicholas 3, 15, 18–19, 22
Lossky, Vladimir 69
Louth, Andrew 51
Loyer, Olivier 12–13

Massignon, Louis 57
Maximus the Confessor 69–71
Merton, Thomas 57
Methodism 26, 45
Methodist Movement 35, 48
Meyendorff, John 6
Monchanin, Jules 57
Moorman, J. R. H., *The Anglican
  Spiritual Tradition* 3
Mozley, J. B., in *British Critic*, 15, 57

Newman, John Henry 3, 16, 48–62
  passim; *Lectures on Justification*
  51, 53
Nicene creed 36

Outler, Albert 34
Oxford History of English Literature
  (Lewis) 8
Oxford Movement 15, 24, 48–62

Palamas, St Gregory 46, 66
Pantycelyn, William Williams 4,
  24–47, 60; *Aleluia* 40; *Farewell
  Visible, Welcome Invisible
  Things* 43; *Theomemphus* 37
Paul, St (apostle) 29, 61
Pauline teaching 6, 44
Personality, corporate 4, 58–9, 68, 76
Peter, St 14, 51
'Progress our Perfection' (Pusey) 23
Puritan Movement 34
Pusey, Edward Bouverie 3–4, 48–62,
  65–7; 'Bliss of Heaven' 57;
  'Progress our Perfection' 23
Pusey, Lucy 54

Rattenbury, J. Ernest 32, 34
Reynolds, Edwards, bp, *Treatise on the
  Passions and Faculties of the
  Soul* 39

Rowland, Daniel 35
Rublev, Andrei 45, 74
Ruysbroeck 54

St Saviour's, Leeds 53
Schmemann, Alexander 4–5, 63
Second Vatican Council 21, 48
Sense, common 31, 37
Shakespeare 2, 7
Song of Songs 41–2, 44
Staniloae, Dumitru 71, 73
Symeon the New Theologian 46

Tears, gift of 34, 77
Theomemphus (Pantycelyn) 37
Thomas, R. S. 72
Thornton, Martin, *English Spirituality* 3
Tradition 2–3, 34, 36–7, 49, 54, 69

Treatise on the Passions and Faculties of the Soul (Reynolds) 39

Vaughan, Henry 25
von Balthasar, *Herrlichkeit* 46–7, 62

'Weight of Glory' (Lewis) 12
Wesley, Charles 3, 4, 24–47, 50, 69; *Hymns on the Lord's Supper* 29; *Large Hymn Book* 33
Wesley, John 25, 26–7, 36–7, 50, 69; *Large Hymn Book* 30
Williams, John 37
Williams, William, Pantycelyn *see* Pantycelyn

Yin and Yang 65